Girls on the Verge

St. Martin's Griffin New York

Girls on the Verge

*Debutante Dips, Drive-bys,
and Other Initiations*

VENDELA VIDA

To my parents and, of course, Vanessa

Library of Congress Cataloging-in-Publication Data

Vida, Vendela.
    Girls on the verge : debutante dips, drive-bys, and other
initiations / Vendela Vida.
        p.   cm.
    ISBN 0-312-20044-7 (hc)
    ISBN 0-312-26328-7 (pbk)
    1. Young women—United States—Social conditions.   2. Young
women—United States—Psychology.   3. Initiation rites—United
States.   I. Title.
HQ799.7.V53   1999
305.242'0973—dc21   99-26036
                                                             CIP

First St. Martin's Griffin Edition: June 2000

10 9 8 7 6 5 4 3 2 1

AUTHOR'S NOTE

In writing this book I've changed the names and some of the distinguishing characteristics of the young women (and men) who are under twenty-one years of age. My decision to make these alterations was two-fold. In some cases, identifying them could land them in harmful situations with their parents, teachers, or peers. And, because they made their decisions as minors, I didn't believe they should be forever held accountable for them. None of the people who appear in the following pages, however, are fictional or composite characters, and real names have been used for all adults.

Venus is kind to creatures young as we;
We know not what we do, and while we're young
We have the right to live and love like gods.

—Ovid,
The Metamorphoses, Book IX

How easily, how recklessly we join this group or that, religious, political, theatrical, intellectual—any kind of group: that most potent of witches' brews, charged with the possibilities for harm and for good, but most often for illusion.

—Doris Lessing,
Love, Again

CONTENTS

INTRODUCTION

Sand Castles

I'm standing outside a chapel in Las Vegas talking to girls—some of whom are barely sixteen—who are about to say their till-death-do-us-parts. Suddenly, I can't take it any more. What's getting to me isn't the days I've spent listening to these quasi-child brides' stories that make the poet Philip Larkin's line "They fuck you up, your mum and dad" seem like a universal truth, but the heat. It's July and this is the desert and I can actually see the sun's rays—they look like sparks from Apollo's chariot.

I go back to my hotel, the Rio, to swim and cool off. The Rio has three pools, two shaped like shells and one shaped like a fish. The shallow end of the conical shell–shaped pool washes up on a sand shore, and there on the makeshift beach I recognize a young couple (he: twenty; she: eighteen) I've interviewed at a wedding chapel earlier in the day. Apparently, they're starting off their honeymoon by trying to build a sand castle with nothing but their hands. The groom, with blue surfer shorts and a pimply back, diligently works on constructing a bridge, but a structural engineer he is not; his various attempts cave into the castle's moat. The new bride, gaunt and sunburnt in an orange bikini, repeatedly tries to fashion a castle tower out of sand, only to have it crumble.

Throughout the course of writing this book, the image of this young bride's plight has stayed with me like an ever-present photograph, in part, I suppose, because it captures my vision of many of the young women I've met who are undergoing initiation rituals today. They, too, are marooned on the shores of adulthood, without tools or training or even a firm foundation on which to build their lives.

This wasn't always the case—neither with young women nor initiation rituals. And this is the crux of this book: why traditional initiation rituals are no longer suiting young women's needs and how, in turn, young women today are embracing new rituals that, while instantly gratifying, may in the long term prove to be merely expressions of their youth, like the young bride's sand castle.

Arnold van Gennep, whose 1908 book *The Rites of Passage* coined the phrase, wrote that transitions from one age to another, from one occupation to another, are implicit in the very fact of existence. Often, he wrote, these rites of passage are marked by ceremonies "whose essential purpose is to enable the individual to pass from one defined position to another that is equally well defined." These ceremonies are what we call rituals.

Of course, initiation rituals are nothing new. Among ancient cultures, initiations were performed when a child had physically attained adulthood—which in the case of females meant when a girl had her first period. At that point, the girl had to endure tests and trials to prove her maturity. Those girls who passed the tests were treated as adults within the community.

Even today, in other cultures female coming-of-age rituals almost exclusively concern a young woman's sexuality. Clitoridectomies and infibulations (the sewing together of the lips of the vagina) are still performed in some countries, most notably African, to ensure three things, according to Esther Hicks in her book *Infibulation: Female Mutilation in Islamic Northeastern Africa*: "that a girl is a virgin when she first marries (and therefore qualifies for marriage), that her sexuality has been controlled, and that it is unlikely she will have extramarital affairs. If a girl is not 'purified' through circumcision," Hicks continues, "she may not marry, bear children, and 'attain a position of respect in later years.' "

In Pygmy culture, a girl's first period symbolizes that she is a woman and is cause for a celebratory ritual, the *elima*. Near the end of the month-long *elima* feast, the men in the village try to fight their way into the *elima* hut. The winner, the man who succeeds in getting in first, spends a night with the recently initiated woman to see how they get along in bed, and if all goes well, makes her his wife. In Western cultures, even as recently as the 1950s (and maybe still in the minds of some parents), the debutante ball celebrated a girl's nascent sexuality and readiness for marriage and childbearing.

But for the most part in America today, time and feminism have liberalized sexual mores; therefore, the need to assert a young woman's virginity and childbearing status via ritual has become less important. In a sense, yesterday's coming of age rituals that inducted young women into adulthood based on sexual development are to-day's initiation rituals—ones that seek to secure adult identities that have less to do with first menstruation or the loss of virginity and more to do with personal choice. Postfeminism, young women have myriad options of what they want to do with their lives and who they want to be. Yet with this newfound freedom also comes a new sense of confusion. Adolescent girls today reach this point of transition in their lives at a time when our culture's expectations for women have probably been permanently fragmented.

A recent editorial in *Bust*, a 'zine for young women written by young women, put it this way:

When Freud asked his classic question, "What do women want?" he seemed to think that the answer was some kind of deep, dark secret that we chicks were just keeping to ourselves. But the whole problem is that we women don't really *know* what we want. I mean, how could we? We are given so many conflicting messages about what's expected from us—what we're supposed to look like (as fragile and beautiful as Kate Moss, as pneumatic and crass as Pamela Lee, as sexually aggressive as Little Kim and as sexually demure as Jewel), [and] what we're supposed to do . . . that it's extremely difficult to find a place that we can fit into comfortably.

As social and familial cohesion have decreased, the need for a comprehensible and well-defined place in the world (a set of attitudes/dress codes/morals, etc.) has increasingly gone unmet. As a result, young women have adapted, created, or embraced rituals to help formulate their identity—rituals that help them order their experiences and relationships in an increasingly chaotic culture.

Contemporary female initiation rituals differ from their male counterparts because, first, boys have historically had more choice as far as identities are concerned, whereas for girls, this same freedom and range of possibilities is something novel; it used to be that her available roles were circumscribed primarily to wife, mother, homemaker. Second, according to Carol Gilligan, author of *In a Different Voice* and the first holder of a chair in gender studies at Harvard's School of Education, boys are more at risk in early childhood, when cultural norms pressure them to separate from their mothers, whereas girls are more at risk psychologically in adolescence. Gilligan writes, "From the different dynamics of separation and attachment in their gender identity formation through the divergence of identity and intimacy that marks their experience in the adolescent years, male and female voices typically speak of the importance of different truths, the former of the role of separation as it defines and empowers the self, the latter of the ongoing process of attachment that creates and sustains the human community."

"Oh! What a happy time you are at," Anna exclaims to Kitty in Tolstoy's *Anna Karenina*. "I remember, and I know that blue haze like the mist on the mountains in Switzerland. That mist which covers everything in that blissful time when childhood is just ending, and out of that vast circle, happy and gay, there is a path growing narrower and narrower, and it is delightful and alarming to enter the ballroom, bright and splendid as it is. . . . Who has not been through it?"

Simply put, rituals are a way for young women to find their way out of the mist.

While researching this book I spoke with hundreds of young women across the country, age thirteen and up, about initiation rituals into both adulthood and identity. Whenever possible, I studied these rituals in the locale in which they seemed most prominent or had some history; for example, I observed young brides in Las Vegas, Nevada, and witches in Salem, Massachusetts. I was struck by the prominence of traditional rituals like the debutante ball—a ritual that the debutantes themselves acknowledged as anachronistic, something they usually claimed to do to please their parents.

Equally remarkable was the metamorphosis of a number of more traditional rituals like sorority initiations and the Latin American ritual of the *quince*, which now bear only the slightest resemblance to their original incarnations. Rather than being modified and modernized to suit the contemporary needs of girls today, *quinces* have been reduced from a significant cultural ritual with religious resonances to an excuse for girls to pose for Lolita-esque portraits on their fifteenth birthday; sorority initiations, which once upon a time inducted young college women into literary societies, have devolved into beauty and popularity contests.

Of course, rituals have always evolved and/or devolved. So it's not surprising that older rituals that may have centered on sexuality and social control have become more about helping young women establish an identity per se, and that young women would turn to these rituals to carve out new identities for themselves. I find it interesting, however, that many of the least traditional paths chosen by women—whether it's a gang girl or a witch practicing Wicca or a young bride—all entail being initiated into a group that fulfills the same needs in their lives as more traditional rituals. Sororities and girl gangs provide their members with a sense of sisterhood. Like the *quince*, which originally sought to establish a connection with a culture and a religion, Wiccan initiations induct girls into a past culture—Celtic—and a faith. And while the original purpose of a debutante ball was for a wealthy family to introduce a young woman into a class-restricted marriage market so she could start a family, young brides getting married today often do so to create the family they never had growing up.

"I am unlike anyone I have ever met. I will venture to say I am like no one in the whole world. I may be no better, but at least I am different." So wrote Rousseau on the first page of his *Confessions*. While young women in search of identities today may claim they want to assert their individuality by taking on an extreme identity, this is not wholly accurate. They want to be different from *most* people, but certainly not from everyone in the whole world: a girl practicing Wicca wants to be able to say "I'm a witch" and shock people on subways into changing seats; a gang girl wants to be able to say "I'm a Blood" and know, and let others know simply by wearing red, that she has a family that is more dangerous than most. There's an ease in taking on an identity that's already been defined; before you're even initiated, you know who your friends will be . . . as well as your enemies, you know where you'll be accepted and where you won't.

What's not included:
During the past couple of years I've talked with many young women who had recently come out as lesbians, and I attended a number of bisexual and lesbian club meetings at colleges ranging from Berkeley to Bard. I had hoped to include their coming-out experiences in the following pages because, especially in certain parts of the country, these young women exhibit such courage and face great challenges— not the least of which includes being disowned. But I found that while coming out to their friends and families was often a major part of coming out as lesbians, there was no set ritual, no ceremony, that a girl had to go through to become a lesbian.

This may sound obvious, but it's an important point to make because I have been asked why I'm not including girls getting their first jobs or moving away from home. While these may be rites of passage, there is no prescribed ritual: It varies from individual to individual. When a person chooses to go through a ritual, he or she knows the terms of agreement—that is, what one's identity will be and what new privileges he or she will have earned after going through the ceremony. Rituals are, after all, ritualistic: They have a history, they'll have a future, and they have an established, albeit often modified, meaning, even if it is only established and understood within the group or community into which one is being inducted. To put it plainly, a girl can identify herself as a lesbian or go to college without undergoing a ritual, whereas a girl cannot join a sorority without going through rush, nor become a bride without going through a wedding ceremony.

Similarly, I have been asked why I don't consider tattoos or body pierces rituals. My answer is "because they're not." I know one young woman who got her navel pierced to symbolize that she had finally, after eighteen years, severed the umbilical cord binding her to her mother; I know another who wanted to get a tattoo with the name of her aborted child across her stomach as a ritual that would mean her mourning period for the lost child was finally over. But the meaning of body pierces and tattoos varies; it is not a group-sanctioned process but a personal choice.

Another image that has stayed with me throughout the writing of this book with the same tenacity as that of the sand castle-buildng bride is the image of myself at age fifteen, getting my first fake ID.

"We're here for IDs," I said to the man who stood behind the counter, scooping ice cream in a parlor in a part of San Francisco my parents wouldn't have wanted me going to. He barked a few words to someone else in another language and my two friends and I were quickly ushered to the back, behind a tattered green blanket that hung, like a shower curtain, from hoops on a rod. After filling out forms stating what we wanted our cards to read, my friends and I relipsticked our mouths with Wet 'n' Wild Fire Engine Red lipstick and posed with our "adult" faces—no schoolgirl smiles for us—as the camera's flash sparked like a giant firefly.

While I waited for my proof to be laminated, to be made official, I thought of what was on the other side of the curtain: rainbow sherbet and waffle cones, the sugary treats of youth. By moving beyond the green blanket, I decided, I had crossed a threshold, and this seemed to be confirmed ten minutes later when I held my new identity in my hand. The ID card said that my name was Kaluha West (Kaluha—the sugary treat of adulthood—was my favorite drink, West had the assurance of direction), I was twenty-two (I thought claiming to be twenty-one would be too "obvious"), I was an inch taller than I really was (I'd always wanted to be taller), and I lived at 67 Chattanooga Street. I wasn't even sure there was a Chattanooga Street in San Francisco, but I'd often listened to my parents' Glenn Miller recording of "Chattanooga Choo Choo" and liked the sound of it. I held my ID with its sharp edges tightly in my palm and stared at it like it was a trophy I'd won rather than something I'd bought with five dollars of babysitting money.

I tell this story to let you know where I'm coming from. I'm not an anthropologist. I was recently a teenage girl myself, desperate to be an adult because I wanted what I perceived to be the accompanying privileges—the ability to get into clubs, to buy alcohol from local Mom and Pop stores. But whatever getting a fake ID did for me, one thing it did not do was give me a new identity. It merely served as my passport into adulthood—that is, until it was confiscated at a club when I was seventeen, leaving me back where I started: underage and denied access. For this book I interviewed girls on the verge of womanhood, on the verge of belonging, who underwent rituals that they hoped would give them new identities that were not fake or ephemeral, but everlasting and adult, rituals that would leave their childhoods in the dust.

PART ONE

Family Approved

CHAPTER ONE

Rush: Sorority Sisters

It's the first day of sorority rush at UCLA and things are going smoothly. I'm in a sorority house chatting with a group of sisters when my fellow rushees and I are herded into the sorority's back room for a slide show. The back room has a ceiling full of brightly colored helium balloons, their ribbons curling like fusilli pasta, and more sorority sisters for us rushees to meet, among them a most unwelcome surprise: Nancy.

Now evidently a sorority sister, Nancy is a girl my little sister grew up with and I recognize her immediately. Standing about ten feet away, she looks right at me and I'm positive a loud air-raid like siren is going to go off, the kind of warning signal sororities must surely have on hand to alert sisters than an impostor is in their midst. I hide my face behind my hair and stick my chest out in her direction so she can see my name tag, which bears the name Katie Wintersen, an alias. Like a lighthouse's beam, Nancy's eyes pan the room, and then cross back again, without stopping on any one rushee's face in particular. So I'm safe, for now at least.

The reason for all of the above—the fear, the alias, my relief at not being recognized—is that I am not a legitimate rush candidate. In fact, I'm not even a UCLA student, but a twenty-six-year-old college graduate who has never been in a sorority. The New England liberal arts college I attended didn't even have sororities. By taking part in this ritual undergone by thousands of college women each year, I'm hoping to better understand the enduring appeal of sororities and to experience what it's like to rush.

Going to college has always struck me as the quintessential American experience—that is, of officially leaving behind what you once were and starting over somewhere else. Yet I've never understood why people who have just arrived at college would renounce their freedom by joining a fraternity or sorority so early in the game. Because rush usually starts before classes do, most students have found their frat or sorority before they've even determined their first semester class schedule.

This wasn't always the case. In their original incarnation (the first sorority was founded in 1851 at Wesleyan College in Macon, Georgia), sororities were open literary societies. Would-be members didn't have to go through the rush process, and girls could belong to more than one sorority at a time. In 1902 sororities came together to form a national organization, the Pan-Hellenic, and it was then determined that girls could "pledge" no more than one sorority; soon after "the entertainment of rushees for a short period before the day of formal invitation," i.e., rush, was made official. Over the years the process of joining a sorority has become more rigorous and cutthroat as sororities have become strictly social in nature. This process seems to be based on so little (looks, musical taste, boys known/dated/slept with) and established in such a short period, (rush lasts one week) and yet sorority bonds often endure a lifetime.

I decided to find out for myself what distinguished a sister in one sorority from that of another, and what each sister's everlasting fealty to her chosen sorority was really about. I chose to rush at UCLA because its rush is known for being particularly superficial—rumors of invisible scales existing beneath the thresholds of each house to weigh entering rushees have been going around for years—and particularly severe: Unlike most schools, it's possible to rush UCLA and not get into any sorority.

When I arrive in the L.A. airport on a late September Sunday morning, I find myself ducking surfboards swung around like helicopter propellers by blond, tan boys. Quite a change from last night's party in Manhattan where slow-moving, cigarette-smoking boys immodestly "summarized" at considerable length the plots and importance of their eternally in progress, self-defined Proustian novels, and jousted over interpretations of Joyce. But there's no time to ponder this difference between boys on opposite coasts nor to attend to my lingering hangover; the information that I—or rather, Katie Wintersen—was faxed informs me I have to get to a Welcome Reception for all fall rushees that afternoon.

In the LAX restroom I change from the all-black outfit I'm still wearing from the night before into a multicolored skirt and tank top (this is, after all, L.A.). I gloss my lips with pink—college girls are always wearing pink lipstick and always with a sheen of gloss—and practice smiling in front of the too-brightly-lit airport bathroom mirror. I almost don't recognize my own reflection—in my preparation for rush week I've highlighted my hair (again, this is L.A.), lost a little weight (don't think those rumors of invisible scales didn't get to me) and there's the sought-after Sorority Smile spreading across my face, straining my mouth muscles. I head off for the reception.

The affair is held outside, on one of the student center's terraces, and is attended by representatives from every sorority (they're all wearing light blue T-shirts with the name of their sorority on the front) and girls who hope one day to be like the girls in the light blue T-shirts. Katie Wintersen mills around anxiously with the four hundred some girls in the latter category.

It's hot out, so I go to pour myself some punch at a refreshment table on the edge of the terrace. A mistake. When I turn around I see that in the brief time my back was turned groups have started to congeal, improbably tight cliques of girls heading in different directions—all of which are away from me. I'm worried that my inability to *besister* from the outset will make me an outcast during rush.

Feeling increasingly desperate, I walk over to the girl who's standing closest to me. She looks friendly enough, so I say: "Does everyone tell you you look like Renée Zellweger?"

"Oh my God!" she says. "That's such a compliment." She beams.

Score. I feel like a sleazy fraternity brother on the late-night make.

Her name is Robin and the thing is, she really does look like Renée Zellweger. Robin's about my height—five six—and has below-the-shoulder straight blondish brown hair. Her dark blue eyes seem to take in everything around her without being the slightest bit distracted from our conversation. Her composure and lack of nervous gesturing make her seem more sophisticated than the other rushees who, at any given moment, are either shifting from one foot to the other, consulting a mirror stashed in their purses, or inserting or removing Care Free sugarless chewing gum.

Robin asks why I transferred schools (I say I'm a junior transfer because trying to pass for a freshman when I'm twenty-six seems like a stretch) and I try out my bogus bio. "I grew up in New York," I lie, "and then I went to Columbia, which was only blocks away from my parents." I roll my eyes. "I've always wanted to live in L.A., and I figured college is a good time to experiment, like, living somewhere else." (The frequent interjection of *like* was one of my primary exercises while practicing Sorority Speak during the days before rush.)

"Plus," I continue—lying has never been so easy—"my boyfriend of two years and I just broke up and it was a really bad breakup— we had all the same friends and everything and I realized I could either start over at Columbia, which would be a drag, or, like, start over somewhere else."

"That's so brave of you, Katie," Robin says. I smile. The reason I've made up the story about the break-up is because I know that love is the *lingua franca* of girls and, I imagine, especially of soror-ity sisters. Plus, I don't want them to think the reason I switched schools was because of something in their minds much worse than heartbreak: not having many friends. The reason I claim to have transferred from Columbia is because, having gone to grad school there, I'm familiar with details about the college and its environs—i.e., local bars, its Greek system, and, should it come up, the course curriculum—details that make lying easier and less spurious sounding.

When I ask Robin where she's from she says, "You've probably never heard of it, but I'm from Pacifica." Pacifica! I can't believe it. Pacifica is a small town outside of San Francisco where I was raised until I was four, when my family moved into the city. Of course, I can't tell Robin this and I feel a certain sorrow in not being able to reveal our shared roots.

In part because I've taken on an alter ego myself, and in part because I feel an affinity for Robin, I find myself imagining she is the person I would have been had my family stayed in Pacifica. This identification with Robin makes me start to think that maybe rush is a reasonable—albeit hastened—approximation of how friend-ships naturally evolve. I chose to approach Robin on the basis of looks, vibe, and proximity—all superficial motivations, yes, but though only I know it, we have something substantial in common and she's definitely a likable person. Maybe, I think, these sorority friendships only seem arbitrary.

At the end of the reception I make my way over to the registra-tion table. I fill out a sorority rush registration card, fabricating everything. Since I don't know how many digits are in UCLA stu-dent ID numbers, I peer over another rushee's shoulder, but she notices my glances and shields her form the way people do when they think you're cheating. Nonetheless, I manage to determine how many numbers are in an ID, give the name of a New York high school many of my friends attended (Stuyvesant), and explain that

I've transferred from Columbia, where, I claim, my activities included writing a men's fashion column for the school paper.

When turning in my form and forking over twenty dollars (thankfully I don't have to write a check), I'm informed that the next day will be a long, ten-party day.

"What should I wear?" I ask the girl with heavily waxed eyebrows who's taken my money.

"Well, be comfortable," she says, "but wear what you want to rush in." She smiles a conspiratorial *Get it?* smile that implies what she really means to say is, "Wear what you want to be judged and evaluated in, dress like your popularity/ happiness/ overall success while you're at UCLA, and maybe the rest of your life, too, depends on it."

On Monday morning, rush officially begins. Classes don't start until Thursday, so for three days rush is a full-time job, or rather, a full-time audition. This year's UCLA rush theme is "Come As You Are." Glancing around at orientation I note that the rushees are all smarter than to show up au naturel. Dressed in trendy patterned miniskirts and spaghetti-strapped tank tops, or little sundresses and heels, and with every strand of hair blow-dried, they look as though they're headed for a night of dates that entail drinking and dancing rather than a day of house tours. Strange when you consider that no boys are present at rush and that during rush week rushees are prohibited from going to fraternity parties (sorority sisters who have been elected as "advisors" to the rushees frequent the frat parties to ensure rushees don't violate this rule). Not so strange when you realize that female attractiveness to males is a primary consideration in sorority rush. The rushees are primped so that they will look like the kind of girls boys like, and therefore the sisters will select them because this will bring benefits to the house: Attractive rushees improve, or at least maintain, the sorority's gene pool, and therefore its reputation as well.

At check-in I am given a name tag and a rush identification number (390). The 430 rushees are divided into ten groups that rotate among ten sorority houses. On the first day we will go to ten thirty-five-minute parties, one at each of the houses. I'm in Group 10 with all the other rushees whose last names fall at the end of the alphabet. All groups have two group leaders, or Rho Chis as they're called. (The *Chi* is pronounced with a hard *K* sound, as in the Greek.) My group leaders are named Claire and Celerie, and they're members of sororities, but they're not allowed to tell us which ones they're in because they are supposed to be impartial and not influence our decisions. (When visiting the houses I see that each sorority has taped black paper over photographs of some of their members. At first, I think this means that the person who appears in the picture has dropped out, died, or gone obese, but I later learn that the purpose of the paper is to veil which Rho Chis are members of which sorority.)

Rho Chis are the bearers of bad news—they call and comfort rushees if they're not invited to join any sororities. Theirs are the shoulders we are supposed to cry on if we don't get invited back to our favorite house. Like the best-prepared camp counselors, Rho Chis carry emergency kits with them at all times. Their kits include tampons, mints, Band-Aids (all the brand new high-heeled shoes leave the rushees with multiple blisters), and nail polish (to halt a run in a rushee's stocking). This last item seems particularly anachronistic, a leftover from a time when bare legs were considered improper, a time before bare legs were a valuable asset in flaunting minimal fat content and a good tan. Only one girl in Group 10 is wearing stockings, I notice, and she must notice this too, because after only ten minutes she's excused herself to go to the restroom and returns with newly exposed limbs.

Before we head off for our first party, Claire and Celerie have us play a name game of the variety you play in camp when you're seven. The particular name game we're forced to play is one in which the group pretends we're all going on a picnic and we each pack an item that starts with the same first letter as our name. Example: Claire's going on a picnic and she's packing cheese; Celerie's going on a picnic and she's packing celery.

Even an innocuous-seeming exercise like the picnic game makes it clear who's going to get into a sorority and who's not. (Lesson: Nothing in rush is innocuous.) A girl with hay-colored hair who looks like she could be on a milk commercial announces, "My name is Hillary and I'm going on a picnic and I'm going to pack hummus." We're sitting on stairs in front of a lecture hall and fellow rushees on the stairs below and above me murmur, "That's so healthy," as though (a) what's really cool about Hillary is that she's a health freak, and (b) we're actually going on a picnic.

Next, a girl whose lip gloss seems to reflect the morning sun says, "My name is Carol and I'm going to pack kumquats." Her shiny lips smile such an I'm-proud-of-myself-for-saying-something-original smile that I don't have the heart to voice my opinion that her answer should be disqualified on the basis of poor orthography. (Lesson Number 2: Rush brings out a competitive edge in people.)

Unlike the other rushees, I have the disadvantage of not having played this game with the same name since childhood. The reason I chose the alias Katie is two-fold: (1) I've always wanted a name people could pronounce without being instructed three times, and (2) a friend of mine who lives in L.A. is named Katie and said I could list her voice-mail number (which has an outgoing message saying "Hi, this is Katie . . .") as my own. Wintersen I chose because it sounded sufficiently nonethnic, which, considering the homogeneity in the sorority system, may have turned out to be a good choice. Ethnically speaking, UCLA is a diverse school. Yet while only 35 percent of the university's student body is Caucasian (40 percent is Asian; 18 percent is African American), the Greek system is a reservoir of whiteness. Asian and African American sororities do exist at UCLA, but students wishing to join them don't go through the official Pan-Hellenic rush.

I'm still wishing I had picked a first name that was more amenable to the picnic game when it's my turn. I haven't thought of anything better, and I'm craving chocolate, so I say, "My name is Katie and for the picnic I'll bring a Kit Kat." Thankfully, no sorority sisters who can report me are present (at least the Rho Chis aren't *supposed* to report anything), and I view this as a sort of practice Social Aptitude Test and make a mental note to study up on my nonfattening *K* foods. Does Special K count? I wonder.

Poor Deborah, though. At well over two hundred and fifty pounds and wearing what resembles a mud-colored muumuu more than a Sorority Sister Sundress, she pipes up with considerable confidence, "My name is Deborah and for our picnic I'm going to pack Doritos." Her test run does not bode well for her. I can imagine a sorority sister looking at her and thinking, *fat, dandruff, glasses,* and I feel bad that she's not going to get what she thinks she wants.

One of the first houses Group 10 goes to is Kappa Kappa Gamma, reputed to have all the pretty girls, cocaine parties, and strict bulimia regimens for its members who are failed anorexics. Our Rho Chis escort us to the bottom of the house's brick steps and we wait until the party officially starts. Up and down Hilgard—the street where all the sororities are lined up like pastel-painted, front lawn–mowed, floral-pattern draped, Martha Stewart–esque suburban homes—the other groups are similarly clustered, waiting for the doors of sisterhood to open.

At the appointed time, the president and rush chair come out and welcome us to Kappa Kappa Gamma. They are both blond, and the bright sun reflecting off their heads makes it look like they're wearing crowns. I'm not the only one to note what a vision they are; one fellow rushee standing near me lets out an "Oh my God!" as though some nonminor deities have just appeared to her in person.

I get in line with the other rushees in my group and shake hands with the president and the rush chair at the door. I say, "Hi, I'm

Katie," and they say, "Welcome to Kappa Kappa Gamma, Katie." Then another girl greets me, gets me a glass of water with a semicircular slice of lemon wedged onto the rim, and walks me to a table in the house's garden where yet another girl is sitting. She introduces us, and before leaving me, takes my calling card. On the first day I have ten calling cards (one for each party) that my Rho Chis have given me and on which I've written "Katie Wintersen" and my rush ID number.

The girl at the table is named Tina and she starts the conversation by asking where I'm from, what year I am, why I transferred, what I think of L.A., and what my major is. After three minutes another sister comes over and squats near us—actually, it's more like a curtsey—and Tina introduces us to each other. "Julie, this is Katie. Katie was just telling me that she wants to be an English major." "Oh really!" Julie says, as though this is very exciting. "Katie," Tina says, "I'm going to leave you now to talk with Julie but it was nice meeting you." Julie then talks to me about my major, where I'm from, what year I am, why I transferred, and what I think of L.A. After three minutes with Julie, Alyssa comes over and asks what we're talking about.

The banality of these conversations with the sorority sisters isn't entirely their fault. Sorority sisters actually have to attend "conversation skills workshops" at which they are trained in how to make a rushee feel comfortable and instructed not to ask any potentially embarrassing or emotional questions. Emotional questions include anything about the rushee's home (she might get homesick) or anything about her boyfriend (a Kappa Kappa Gamma at Northwestern told me that conflicts have been known to arise when a sister asks a rushee who her boyfriend is, only to discover that they're both dating the same guy). But just as striking as the similarity of all their conversational initiatives is the uniformity of their appearances: With the hollowed cheeks of Modigliani women, all the Kappas seem to share the same hairstyle, dress, diet, earrings, perfume, and toenail polish, not to mention an equal amount of sun-kissed freckles sprinkled on the bridges of their small noses, some of which are surely rhinoplastic. I get the feeling that, unlike their highly honed, interchangeable small talk, no extensive workshopping or training is necessary to ensure their physical homogeneity.

The game of greet-judge-pass-the-rushee continues until I sit down for a longer conversation with Ashley, a tall sophomore who has pink glitter on her face and in the valley of the V created by the neckline of a thin pink T-shirt designed to show off her ample chest. She asks if I have any questions for her, and so I ask what she likes about Kappa.

"I like that we can be really silly together. I mean, we like partying, but there's also school. But you're seeing us at our most sophisticated side, I mean, we're *talking* and everything."

Someone announces that the entertainment is about to begin.

"Oh my God," Ashley says. "Aren't you excited?"

"Sure," I say, and sit up straighter and try to look wide-eyed.

The entertainment at Kappa features a girl less attractive than the other sisters, dressed up as a Loser-Looking Rushee who's just arrived at UCLA and wants to join Kappa. (I wonder if the choice to have her play the part was a deliberate one.) She watches the Kappa sisters dance to "YMCA" and "Celebration," but when she tries to dance with the best of them she's laughed at. She perseveres, however, and after shedding her glasses and bookbag and literally following the other girls' footsteps throughout the "I Will Survive" number she, too, is given a pink scarf and made into a Kappa. The pink scarf is tied around the rushee's neck in the style of the Pink Ladies in *Grease*. The allusion to this elitist group is not accidental.

The entertainment emphasizes two things: (1) humiliation is part of the rush process, and (2) Toni. Toni is the president of Kappa Kappa Gamma and she looks as though before doing dance performances here she was on *Beverly Hills, 90210*. She's thin, blond, large-breasted, and is never not smiling. She's also never not dancing. Just when you think she's burned out from kicking her long legs up in the air like a Rockette and has retreated off stage for good she improbably returns for the next song in a new outfit, her legs kicking even higher.

All the sisters are cheering Toni on, but Ashley is the most enthusiastic of them all. She's clapping to the music and screaming "Go, Toni" and "Shake it, Toni." I look around to see if the other rushees are clapping or shouting; they're not. I'm momentarily relieved by this and feel my lack of enthusiasm is excusable. But then, upon scanning the garden a second time, I notice that there's a reason the other rushees aren't clapping or screaming: They've been mesmerized by this potent display of sexuality and sorority spirit. I can see it in their eyes, which look like they've been dappled with Kappa Glitter.

When the dance performance is (finally) over, Ashley says, "Did you like it?"

"Yeah," I say. I know that I haven't exhibited the proper enthusiasm. But Ashley, possibly softened by the rushee's plight she just witnessed in the show, gives me one more chance. She looks around at all her sisters and says, "This morning was such a trip. You should have seen us. We were all running around listening to music and going through each other's drawers and closets getting dressed together. I helped make the decision that everyone should wear bright colors." Ashley brings her hands to her heart, and squeals (yes, she squeals), "I just *love* colors. Colors make me *so* happy. What's your favorite color?"

"Excuse me?" I say. I'm surprised to still be surprised by the strangeness of being in an environment where the reflective/refractive properties of light can be loved . . . and where that love/nonlove is judged.

She gives me a never-mind-I-shouldn't-have-asked look. Sternly silent, she walks me to the entryway I came through, which is now dark with flashing lights—the desired effect is that it's like a model's runway, the flashes those of cameras snapping away. Maybe there really are cameras, I think. Maybe pictures are being taken of all the rushees so the sisters can evaluate each girl individually later on. I imagine all the Kappas sitting around a slide show of these candid photos, alternately waving pom-poms for girls they like and throwing lard at the ones they don't.

On either side of the makeshift catwalk Kappas are lined up and they're all saying good-bye. And there's Toni—again, and in a new outfit!—at the front door. I have no idea how she's made it there from the stage through the traffic jam of rushees and sisters so quickly—maybe there's an underground passageway? She's not even breathing heavily.

Before I know it, I've made it outside where it's light and calm. I feel dizzy from the experience.

One of our next parties is at Delta Delta Delta. At the set time, like a bird shooting out of the door of a cuckoo clock, the Tri-Delt rush chair and president exit their house as one, holding hands. They say how excited all the girls are to meet us, and welcome us in "without further ado." Once inside, it's greet-judge-pass all over again . . . until I meet Kim. Kim is a beautiful funkily-dressed black Tri-Delt (the first funkily-dressed, not to mention black woman I've seen during rush) whose bookshelf—which I see when she takes me on a house tour—is not to be believed. Unlike bookshelves at other sororities that seem to serve as no more than display cases for teddy bears holding UCLA banners and photos of smiling sorority sisters with gold-embossed captions saying "Sisters" or "Best Friends," Kim's bookshelf houses an impressive collection of Scandinavian literature. So Kim and I talk Laxness and Lagerkvist, Hamsun and Ibsen, and I think/dream/hallucinate that maybe sororities still have a trace of the literary society in them. Not even members of my mother's Swedish Women's Group with all their eating of lutfisk and dancing around midsummer poles have ever discussed Lagerkvist with me.

I talk with Kim until it's time for the Delta Delta Delta slide show. The main purpose of the sororities' slide shows is to showcase the sisters' popularity among fraternity boys. By the time the slide show starts, you've met some of the girls in the house, and ostensibly you've been sizing each other up. But because rushees can't go to fraternity parties during rush week (the sisters aren't allowed to go to frat parties during rush week, either, which may account for some of their excessive energy), rushees don't get a chance to see the sisters being hugged/courted/liquored up by the fraternity boys. So the not-so-subliminal message of Tri-Delt's slide show, which features cute boys dancing with Tri-Delt girls at date parties, kissing their Tri-Delt girlfriends at mixers, and boys pinning Tri-Delt sisters (pinning is a Greek ritual between a fraternity brother and a sorority sister that signifies that the couple will soon be engaged) is this: The right boys (i.e., good-looking, cool-dressing, openly affectionate members of "good" fraternities) like Delta Delta Delta girls.

I have to say it's effective. I find myself slipping into my role as Katie Wintersen who has just broken up with her long-term boyfriend and is on the rebound. Maybe, I think, if I become a Tri-Delt I'll go out with these alpha males as well. Not only that, but I'll get Tri-Delt sweatshirts to authenticate and advertise my membership to everyone around me and a social calendar that includes bid day, pledge night, dad's day, and semiformals. It's not a social calendar alone I covet, but the social calendar of a group. All serious groups have their own calendars, just as religions do, and the true sign of belonging to a group, I've decided, is that you plan the rest of your life around the group's events.[1]

---

[1]It's worth noting here that later in the week when I have the dubious honor of going into a fraternity house I learn that, somewhat unsurprisingly, during fraternity rush there are no slide shows, and no organized small talk. In fact, in comparison to sorority rush, fraternity rush seems positively civilized. Fraternity rush consists of informal hanging out and talking about whatever you want. Another difference: While the sororities' slide shows feature all the *fun* they have with the fraternity brothers, and many of the sorority sisters' rooms prominently display silver-framed photos of sisters and their fraternity brother dates at formals, the most common photographs I see in fraternity guys' rooms, and especially in the fraternities' dining rooms, are of a decidedly different nature.

At the end of the slide show the girls form a semicircle around all the seated rushees, lock hands, and sing along with the 10,000 Maniacs' "These Are Days." They keep singing, a cappella, even after the song is over, and suddenly I feel hope swelling up like a balloon around Katie Wintersen's recently broken heart. Friends to break into song with, days to remember—what could be better medicine for the lovelorn, or for those whose first time it is away from home, for anyone? UCLA already feels smaller, less foreign. If I make it through sorority rush, I think, I will have a place to live, a full social calendar, and a hundred-plus friends—sisters, no less. All within a week. Life has never been so easy.

At the end of the long day of parties, Group 10 reconvenes with our Rho Chis, who instruct us in filling out our preference slips. We are to put down our top seven choices—my top choice is unquestionably Tri-Delt—and when the houses put down their top choices of rushees, the computer will determine a schedule for the next day. The omnipotent computer is ominously referred to as "the scantron." Whenever the word *scantron* is mentioned during rush week even the most composed of rushees can be seen chomping on their French-manicured nails.

On Tuesday Group 10 meets on the steps by the inverted—like an innie belly button—fountain at 9:15. I'm still exhausted from the approximately three hundred conversations I had the day before—or rather, from having had more or less the same conversation with three hundred people. There's a problem with one of the schedules, Claire tells us, and Celerie is waiting at the Pan-Hellenic office to find out what's wrong.

Convinced that the problematic schedule is mine, I start to sweat. Even this early in the morning, the sun is streaming onto the

---

The majority showcase the brothers on spring break in Mexico holding Coronas and, on their shoulders, carrying bikini-clad, seemingly non-UCLA women.

pavement, leaving not the slightest slice of shade. It's as though someone's put peaches under each of my armpits and, like a juice presser, I'm squeezing out sticky juice that runs down the sides of my body and into the waistband of my skirt. I'm sitting next to Robin and she's telling me that today is her boyfriend's birthday, and I try to make conversation about what she's gotten him, how they're going to celebrate, etc., but my mind is reeling through possible problems as well as the excuses I can offer the Pan-Hellenic office. I'm not as concerned about punishment as I am about how, given that everyone's so secretive about the process, I'll find out about what goes on during rush if I am "discovered." All the Pan-Hellenic presidents and sorority sisters alike rely on the refrain that rush is "a mutual selection process." An obvious lie.

While we're waiting for Celerie to find out what's wrong with the one missing schedule, Claire tells us that at 9:40 we'll get our lists of parties for the day. The scantron has matched our preference lists with those of the houses and we may have up to seven parties to go to that day, or we may have zero—it all depends on whether or not the houses we "preferenced" also preferenced us. "You guys need to remain quiet when you get your lists—don't get really excited, or ask the person sitting next to you what houses she got—because this is a really emotional time."

Claire is pretty down-to-earth (she's wearing Birkenstocks) and I know from my one day of house parties that she's not in one of the snobby sororities. "Don't be upset if you didn't get invited back to a sorority you really liked," she says. "It doesn't mean that they didn't like you, it just means that they don't think you'll fit in there." She says this with an it's-all-for-the-best attitude.

"Also, if yesterday you talked to a girl at one of the houses and you felt like you really had a good conversation, like you really clicked, and then you're not invited back to that house, don't feel upset with her personally, or feel embarrassed or mad when you see her around campus. It's not all up to the girls you talked to. It's a democratic decision—the whole house decides on who gets asked back—and the girl you talked to and clicked with isn't the only one deciding."

If the people who talked to you aren't necessarily the ones deciding on whether or not you're asked back, this means that the decisions are being made by people who may not have even said hello to you. The harsh reality behind Claire's "comforting" words is that whether or not you're asked back is determined by your looks/dress/mannerisms and what sorority girl A said to sorority girl B about your "conversational skills."

At 9:40 the schedules are distributed to all the groups. I'm amazed to find that they haven't discovered I'm an impostor, and that I have seven parties to go to. I'm surprised and oddly jealous of Katie Wintersen: Had I been acting like myself and not Katie—that is, saying whatever was on my mind and not what I felt I should say, and had I dressed how I felt and not how everyone else did—I wouldn't have been met with such approval. I start imagining how my whole life could have been different had I just not been me.

Not all of the parties are at my number-one ranked houses (no Kappa), but then I reflect on Claire's words of wisdom. I'm consoled by the fact that maybe the girls I talked with enjoyed my conversation; it was just the other girls—the ones I didn't meet—who didn't approve of my appearance.

"Are you happy with what you got?" Robin asks. I look over at her and see that her it's-my-boyfriend's-birthday blush has blanched into a pale shade of death.

"So-so," I say.

"I'm not at all happy," she says, although there's really no need for her to tell me this since she looks positively lachrymose. "I only got invited back to three houses and I'd only consider one of them!"

"Robin," I say, "there must be some mistake." I actually mean this. I'm so enamored of her that I can't imagine why anyone wouldn't be, why everyone isn't. The scantron must be behind this, I think.

And then she says it. "Can I see your list?"

I hesitate. I fumble. I think of telling her that it's for her own good—for the good of our friendship—if she doesn't see it. But her shaky hand is outstretched, her eyes greedy, and I know I have no choice.

Robin looks at it, then she studies it, and then she begins to cry. Not small, movie star–like tears of the sort you'd think a girl like her would cry, a girl who after all looks like a movie star, but mascara-blackened tears that leave skidmark–like trails on her cheeks.

"Robin," I say, "I'm sorry." Suddenly feeling maternal, I stroke her hair. I want to tell her that the only reason I got asked back to more houses is because I was pretending to be somebody I'm not, and she was just being herself. But I know it wouldn't make her feel any better.

"You better go, Katie," she says, and removes my hand from her head. "You have to be at your first party at ten. I don't even have to be anywhere for another hour and a half."

As I leave she starts to cry again, and I say, "Robin . . ."

"Go," she says. She doesn't want my pity; all I want her to know is that I don't think she deserves this fate. It's not that I think sororities are so great, but that I think Robin is, and that sororities should be able to recognize that about her.

My first party is at Delta Delta Delta. It strikes me that all the girls have newly acquired sultry voices of the kind you get from smoking packs a day. But UCLA girls aren't big smokers and it turns out that everyone's throat is hoarse from so much talking—and cheering—the day before. Other than being brought down an octave, the conversations are essentially the same, with one new question thrown into the routine: "Do all the houses seem the same to you?" The correct answer to this question is, of course, "No." Not just "No," but "No, some really stick out above the others in terms of spirit and the quality of the girls." To be *uber*correct, this response must be accompanied by a sufficiently conspiratorial grin. A grin that says, While most houses are *lame*, yours is *cool*. Which is in fact how I feel. Tri-Delt is where Katie Wintersen, as I've created her, would fit in.

As I'm leaving the sisters are all lined up at the door to say good-bye. The obvious purpose of having this departing line is so that if they see a girl they think they "want" they can note her name tag and ID number. This open objectifying of women would be deemed unacceptable if it weren't for the fact that it's all women and this is L.A.

"So good to see you back, Katie," several of the sisters I vaguely remember talking to say as I'm leaving, and I know that they are the reason I'm back, and that they want me to know that they're the reason I'm back. "They're so nice," I write in my notes afterwards—I can't help myself.

At the parties on the second day there are more skits, most of which are based on television shows or movies. At Alpha Delta Pi I have a painful conversation with a cheerleader and watch the sisters perform "We Go Together" from *Grease*, complete with choreographed shimmies. At Chi Omega I watch a Batgirl skit scripted to show off the virtues of a Chi Omega: "A Chi Omega spends fifty to seventy-five percent of her time partying, but she also spends time doing philanthropy and scholasticism," Batgirl says. Anyone who refers to college learning as "doing scholasticism" can't be very good at it, I think.

At Pi Beta Phi there's *another* skit, this one based on *Dick Tracy*. I wonder if the sororities have to register their movie/TV show–themed acts with the Pan-Hellenic office so there aren't any repeats among the houses. But a Pi Phi sister tells me, "I hope you like the skit. We've been doing it for years," and I realize that like clothes inherited from an older sibling, the skits are passed down from year to year. And like hand-me-downs the themes are a little out of date, even if they're supposed to be kitchy. I mean, *Dick Tracy*?

On my way to Theta I see Robin coming down the hill toward me. "Robin," I say, and I grab her hand. "Hi, Katie," she says coolly. She's used her compact to even out the still-remaining red splotches she has on her face from crying. By my estimation, the tears ceased maybe ten minutes before, which means she's been crying for over an hour. She doesn't stop to talk, and I sense that seeing me has set her on the brink of tears again, so I let her hand go, and she continues down the hill.

Cat tails, black noses, and painted whiskers adorn the president, rush chair, and membership chair at Kappa Alpha Theta because the sorority's acronym is KAT. Theta is one of the two sororities known for having the prettiest and thinnest girls (the other is Kappa), and the girls seem proud to look like a coterie of sex kittens.

The girl I'm talking to, Yvonne, asks me what activities I plan to be involved in at UCLA. She asks the question as though she's reading from a cue card behind my head, and for a moment I'm tempted to turn around and see if she is. I quickly sense Yvonne has never read a newspaper in her life, but nonetheless, I tell her about the fashion column for men that I supposedly wrote for the Columbia school paper.

Fortunately (or, at the time it seemed fortunate), just as the cue cards appear to have vanished, the president of the sorority approaches us and introduces herself saying, "Katie, I've heard so much about you and I just wanted to come over and say hello."

She sits next to Yvonne in the shade of an umbrella. Meanwhile, I'm in the sun and I can feel my highlighted hair darkening with perspiration. I smile at her, and wonder to myself what the "so much" she's heard about me could possibly consist of.

"What were you two just talking about?" the president/Queen KAT asks.

"Fashion," Yvonne says, with a flip of her blond hair. (You'd think the flip was intended to punctuate her response if you didn't know that she flips her hair about as often as she blinks.)

"Fashion!" the president gushes. "I just love fashion. I especially love Prada."

"I especially love anything Italian," Yvonne continues.

"I love pasta!" I exclaim, as though we're playing a word association game (which, it turns out, we're definitely not).

Both girls stare at me—not just at me, but more specifically at my thighs. Although my thighs aren't large enough to disqualify me on their own merit alone, I think of how, on the grounds of my response, they could conceivably fear that I'm an agent provocateur sent to fatten them up.

(I did not get asked back.)

That night I hole up in my motel room. When I first checked into my "motor hotel" in L.A. I enjoyed the fact that although close by, it felt worlds away from sorority row. What I've always liked about motels is the feeling of transience they offer, and much to the annoyance of my travel companions I've always opted for the seediest motels, even if better options were available. When I first entered my motel room in L.A., the mattress that sagged like a hammock, the dim lighting, the sound of too-loud TVs pulsing in from other rooms, and the roar of car engines outside the door pleased me greatly. The motel was a welcome respite from the character-free charm of sorority row.

But even as early in rush as Tuesday night it's evident that something has changed in me; both the seedy motel and its social equivalent—crowded, dirty bars and last-minute planning—have lost some of their romantic allure. For the first time, I can identify with Humbert Humbert in *Lolita* when he says he eventually grows "to prefer the Functional Motel—clean, neat, safe nooks, ideal places for sleep, argument, reconciliation, insatiable illicit love." Maybe the appeal of sororities is analogous: clean, neat, safe nooks, ideal places to conduct the business of living, meet dateable boys, and form friendships that all the sorority songs claim will last a lifetime.

On Tuesday night I curl up on my motel room's brown and white velour couch. Styrofoam pops out of the pillow's zippers the way my swollen feet have been spilling out of my strappy high-heeled shoes. I stay up late smoking all the cigarettes I haven't been able to smoke all day, filling the motel room's brown ashtray. With the volume turned down on the flickering television, I talk on the phone. My sister, who was a Kappa at Berkeley but who became disillusioned and deactivated (or as she calls it, "deKappatated"), can't believe I wasn't asked back to Kappa. "What were you wearing?" she asks. She's been on the other side and knows what sorority sisters look for from their rushees.

I talk with a woman I know who was in a sorority at Cornell. She's now thirty and I thought she had a sense of distance, if not humor, about Greek life. "You know," she tells me testily, "you're taking a space away from a girl who might really want to be in a sorority."

I think of Robin and get off the phone as quickly as possible.

I talk to a disgruntled male writer friend of mine who approves of what I'm doing because he doesn't think any blond, peppy, sorority-mold girl would so much as look at him, so he feels that justice is being served, that I'm exposing the same obsession with appearances that would prevent any of these girls from giving him the slightest chance.

I talk to a guy I've been seeing in New York who—although never part of a fraternity or close to that scene—seems to question my coolness when I tell him I wasn't asked back to be a Kappa. Even *he* is well versed in the hierarchy of houses. "What are you going to do if you don't get into a good house?" He sounds worried. He's beginning to have his doubts about me. I'm beginning to question his vanity. I can understand how Katie Wintersen defers to sorority girls' opinions, but I begin to wonder why everyone else does, too—even those who are purportedly against the Greek system seem to give credence and weight to the membership choices of organized groups.

· · ·

Wednesday, I continue to rush. At Alpha Epsilon Phi I see a slide show that's accompanied by songs like "Lean On Me" (for the philanthropy slides), "Groove Is in the Heart" (for the party pictures), and (for the photos of friends) the theme song from Cheers with the lyrics "you wanna be where you can see our troubles are all the same." They obviously haven't bothered to listen carefully to the second verse, which reveals that the song is more about desperation than socialization, "climbing the walls when no one calls; you've lost at love again/And the more you're down and out, the more you need a friend . . ."

At Pi Beta Phi and Delta Gamma I hear tear-jerking stories (stories that bring tears to the sisters' eyes, not mine) from sisters who, like speakers at an Alcoholics Anonymous meeting, stand up and share their experience, strength, and hope . . . about joining their particular sorority. At Pi Beta Phi, the rush chair tells us (jumping up with hands above her head as though shaking pom-poms), "I was in the womb saying 'Go Greek,' " and then adds (hands at her side), "but it's okay if you weren't."

At Delta Gamma the silver-eye-shadowed speaker's story goes like this: "When I was going through rush, I was sitting there like all of you and my leg fell asleep! So when it was time to stand up, I fell backward! But a Delta Gamma sister named Suzie caught me! Suz, will you stand up?" Suzie, a not-dyed blond girl seated in the middle of the room pops up, and her central position and undelayed response remind me that this is the third time she's jumped up for this story today.

All the rushees ooh and aah. Then, they actually applaud Suzie. With tears swelling, the speaker says, "Delta Gamma was there for me then, and they're there for me now."

Later, I ask a DG sister what she likes best about being in a sorority. "I like the mornings the best because we're all in the bathroom blow-drying our hair together? And we ask each other if we have anything in our teeth?"

She says all this in perfect Sorority Upspeak—the transformation of declarative sentences into interrogatives that I know I'll never be able to master. A French teacher once told me that if you learn a foreign language after the age of ten, you'll always have an accent, but if you learn it before, you'll sound like a native of that country. I'm wondering how this DG became fluent in Sorority Upspeak and then she tells me: "All my older sisters, I mean, my real, like, biological sisters, were DGs, too?"

It's not uncommon for a sorority girl to hail from a family of sorority sisters—older sisters, mothers, or grandmothers—and for them all to have been in the same sorority. In fact, while parents ultimately leave the choice of joining a sorority up to the girl, a rushee must get a recommendation letter for every house she rushes from a past member of that house's chapter. This means that rushees at UCLA must track down ten co-workers of their mothers or wives of their father's friends who belonged to chapters of each of the ten sororities at UCLA (it's not imperative that the women belonged to those houses at UCLA—they could have been Delta Gammas at Boulder, Kappa Kappa Gammas at the University of Arizona, or *anything* at the University of Illinois, the only school that has all twenty-six sororities) and convince them to write recommendation letters on their behalf. The letters are sent with photographs of the rushee to all the houses before rush even begins.

Except in Katie Wintersen's case. I don't find out about this letter/photo aspect of rush until I'm in the midst of it—yet another reason I'm scared I'll be "caught." I just hope the sisters are too consumed by skits to be preoccupied with paperwork. What the letter of recommendation requirement emphasizes to me, however, is how instrumental families are in the rush process. Not only do the parents financially support their daughters' desire to be in a house—sororities at UCLA charge membership fees ranging from $1,895 (Kappa Alpha Theta) to $2,237 (Alpha Delta Pi) per member per year on top of the school's $4,050 in-state, $13,034 out-of-state tuition—but they also serve as their social network. After all, what eighteen-year-old female knows ten potential sponsors without brainstorming with her parents about the sorority credentials of everyone they (the parents) know?

That afternoon we have to fill out our forms for pref night. We have to put 1s by our top two choices and 2 and 3 by the others. I sit on the sidewalk and deliberate. Robin puts ones by both her choices (her options, have been winnowed again) and leaves.

I have four houses to choose from—again, not all of them my top choices. What the scantron's print-out tells me is that the lightening of my hair, body, personality, and vocabulary was not extensive or enduring enough. I put down Delta Delta Delta and Kappa Delta as my first choices. The former because it really is where Katie Wintersen would join, and the latter because she has nothing in common with anyone there—all my conversations at Kappa Delta have had the naturalness and suavity of a bad blind date—and I find it amusing that they like Katie. The gamble, of course, is that if I don't get into Tri-Delt, I will end up somewhere I don't want to be, and I'm haunted by the words of the guy I've been seeing: "What are you going to do if you don't get into a good house?" I can't imagine the pressure if I were doing this for real.

One thing that had always intrigued me about sororities before going through rush wasn't that a group of smiling happy girls would associate together—take one look and you'll see that they are always smiling and happy—but rather how those particular smiling, happy girls happened to find each other. Given that they are all happy, why would these young women choose to join, or be chosen to join by, one sorority over another?

Rush week teaches me that some of these girls are happier than others and that sororities function as castes in a social system that is not only reminiscent of high school cliquery, but one that seeks to establish and secure a hierarchy. Throughout the week, fellow rushees have told me which houses they've heard aren't "worth it" to join. They're not talking finances, they're talking about the relative benefits. Some houses are not "worth" joining because they don't do much for your social status or dating life. Another big topic among rushees is what fraternity boys think of the various sororities. A few of the rushees have older brothers who are in fraternities, and rushees defer to these girls for the lowdown.

I put Kappa Delta as my second choice precisely because it is not high on the social ladder and I'm curious to see how it teaches the sisters who end up there—whose first choice may have been compromised more than that of a rushee who ends up at Kappa Kappa Gamma or Kappa Alpha Theta—to smile the Sorority Spirit Smile.

If I really were Katie and I really were planning on joining a sorority at UCLA I would do what is called, in Greek, "committing suicide," or "suiciding." Suiciding is when you just pick one house and pray that they pick you back, otherwise you're not in any house and, as far as the Greek system is concerned, you may as well be dead.

Just before six o'clock Thursday night, three hundred of the remaining rushees show up at one of UCLA's lecture halls for pref night. Pref night means we will go to parties at two of our remaining houses so that we can make a decision (a "preference") about which house we want to join, and the houses can decide if they want us to join. All the girls who weren't asked back to houses were supposed to be called by their Rho Chis during the day so they wouldn't suffer the humiliation of showing up at pref night all dressed up, with literally no place to go. But one rushee who's in a wheelchair shows up in a velvet dress with glitter in her hair and the Rho Chis have to break the bad news to her then and there. "I'm so disappointed," she says, as a Rho Chi wheels her out and back home. Most likely, she would be even more disappointed in the system if she knew the truth: Her Rho Chi later informs me that on the first day she didn't get asked back to any of the houses, so the Pan-Hellenic office made some of the houses invite her back. They just dragged her hopes and her heart along until the very end.

When the rush chair goes up to the podium on the stage at the lecture hall the first thing she does is sigh into the microphone. "You girls all look so beautiful," she says, staring out at the sea of hundreds. She reminds us that pref night will be one of the most emotional nights of our lives. "A way of helping you decide," she continues, "is to think carefully about who talked to you about things that are important to you."

Then we convene with our original groups, and I notice that, unsurprisingly, a lot of faces from the pretend picnic are missing. Seeing eighteen-year-old women dressed up is a bit like seeing a five-year-old girl wearing her mother's blue eye shadow. The rushees' attempts to look older than they are only highlight their youth. Their heels are high and their dresses simulacrums of those featured in fashion magazines, but most carry dark Jansport backpacks—and some even have teddy-bear backpacks—instead of purses. I'm struck with a strange admiration for these girls, who at such a young age go through so much to find a house away from home.

At 6:40 our Rho Chis hand us our schedules for pref night. I have two parties: the first at Delta Delta Delta at 7:00; the next at 8:30 at Kappa Delta. Stopping only to consult their reflections in the windows of parked cars, a stampede of nearly three hundred dressed-up want-to-be sorority girls make their way down Hilgard for the first party. (Those who evidently did not get invited back to their top choices have already absconded the scene, tripping in their high heels as they ran. I consider going after one, a girl whose mother's in the hospital and whose death-bed wish was that her sickness not prevent her daughter from becoming a Theta, but I recall my failure with Robin and opt to let her be.) Tri-Delt is at the bottom of the hill so I have the opportunity to see other rushees standing outside their houses, waiting to be let in. The girls outside Kappa Kappa Gamma are skinny and, judging from their dresses, look like they love colors, too; the girls outside Kappa Alpha Theta look like the kind of girls who would gladly dress up in whiskers and cat tails.

Outside of Delta Delta Delta I meet the other girls who have made it this far. You'd expect us to be sizing each other up like rivals in a beauty pageant given that not all of us will be asked back tomorrow for bid day, when houses invite/don't invite the finalists to join, but instead everyone's full of praise for one another's dress/hair/composure ("you're, like, totally not nervous"). After all, everyone's thinking that we might be in the same pledge class together.

At almost seven exactly the dusky glow gives way to darkness. Tri-Delt's doors open and the sisters stream out, holding candles, singing a sentimental song about sorority sisterhood, as they line up on either side of the stairway.

Next come the dozen or so girls who are welcoming rushees. Carrying a white rose, each of these sisters makes her way past all the other sisters with candles and stops on the third from bottom step. Then she says, "My name is [sister's name here], and I'm especially happy to be welcoming back [rushee's name here] to Delta Delta Delta." The rushee walks up to the sister, is handed the rose, and the two of them hug. In Sorority Speak, the sister who invites a rushee back is the rushee's "silver sister." (In addition to having their own calendars, all groups have their own jargon.) What this means is that she has "preffed" the rushee. Preffed is short for preferenced, and it means that the sister has made a special effort to ensure the rushee is invited back to the house by telling all the other sisters how great the rushee is.

As Kim, lover of all things Scandinavian, descends and stops at the third step, she starts looking around and I try to make eye contact with her, but it's difficult because she's not looking in my direction. She announces that she's "especially happy to be welcoming back . . ." I take a step forward, but she doesn't say "Katie Wintersen" and I feel oddly betrayed. What about Strindberg?, I think.

When Laura, a senior with curly light brown hair, who I talked to the day before about her junior year abroad, welcomes back Katie

Wintersen, I practically skip toward her, get the thornless rose, and give her a hug. I feel elated and popular and wanted. I feel loved. I wonder why I never wanted to be in a sorority before. Like someone who's just gone on Prozac and starts reflecting on how their life would have been different if they had always been that happy, I think about how my life would have been different had I always been surrounded by so much sisterhood. With her arm around me, Laura leads me inside to a table set with a champagne flute filled with sparkling apple juice. We sit at the table and she continues to flatter me and ask me about my/Katie's breakup with my/her boyfriend, and says she's so sorry, that everyone at Tri-Delt is so sorry about this.

When Laura's through, another sorority sister comes and tells me how special I am (I've talked with her for five minutes over the course of the week) until it's time for the ceremony. We move into another room and, guided by our sisters, the other rushees and I form a semicircle around what looks like a big birdbath. Laura stands behind me, rubbing my back with small, clockwise motions. I look around and see that all the silver sisters are rubbing the rushees' backs, and what's more, the other rushees are crying.

The one hundred or so Tri-Delts who aren't preffing girls at the party are lined up around the perimeter of the dim room holding candles. The ones who hold high offices in the sorority—i.e., the president, rush chair, social chair, philanthropy chair, etc.—take turns telling us a "legend" about a girl who stood with a pearl under a crescent moon. To make a long legend short, she made a wish and threw the pearl into the pond, and the ripples from that pearl represent the ripples of friendship that lasted her whole life.

Laura presses a pearl into the palm of my hand and tells me that when it's my turn, I'll go up to the birdbath and put my pearl in, and make a wish. "Don't be nervous," she says. "I'll go with you." Laura, I notice, has tears in her eyes.

So we walk to the birdbath and I throw my pearl in. Of course, everyone assumes your wish is to join Tri-Delt, and this is, in fact, my wish because my heart and Tri-Delt have melded. I concentrate on making the pearl skip like the flat rocks I threw into still lakes as a child. The pearl makes a lot of ripples, and as Laura stares at them, her eyes widen at the sight of what she interprets as an auspicious sign. Then we walk back to the circle, and the other girls throw their pearls in.

When the ceremony is over we all walk down the stairs, accompanied by the singing of Tri-Delts. Outside, all the pledges are ecstatic. "It's like how you feel when you meet a guy," one bubbly girl from Sacramento exclaims, "except it's girls!"

I go to the next house, Kappa Delta, and the woman who's preffing me praises Katie to the roomful of sisters and rushees. "Katie is intelligent, and beautiful, and has so much to offer," she says. I think it's sad, because Katie really wouldn't have anything in common with them and it strikes me that a lot of the girls in the room who are being similarly talked up and praised beyond recognition wouldn't have anything in common with them.

Unlike Tri-Delt, which has a high matriculation rate, Kappa Delta has asked back over fifty girls. They know that they're not at the apex of the caste system and therefore not at the top of everyone's preference list, and don't want to suffer the same fate as a house the previous year which had to "go off campus" (read: die) because it didn't have enough interest and therefore not enough members to "survive."

Early in the week, the flattery consisted of innocuous statements like "I like your earrings," but by pref night things have gotten crazily desperate. "You look just like that girl from 90210," one Kappa Delta says to a rushee who doesn't look like any of the actresses on 90210. The other sisters chirp in that the resemblance is in fact uncanny. Yet when the flattered rushee asks which one she resembles, the sisters are all at a loss.

At the end of pref night, we have to go to a church and write down our preferences. No one's allowed to talk while waiting in line, not even to use their cell phones to call home to their parents. Like Catholics who have the option of going to confession, we're asked if we want to see a counselor in private before making our decision. I decline. I know that Tri-Delt is my first choice.

Outside the church I run into Robin and we go get frozen yogurt together in Westwood. She's found a sorority she likes—the sorority my sister's friend Nancy is in—and my happiness for Robin is genuine because I like her. We compare notes on the evening and she tells me that at her sorority she heard a familiar story about the girl with the pearl and the pond and the crescent moon, and that she too, made a wish. I can't believe it. Her house must have stolen the legend from Tri-Delt, I think. Just wait until I tell the sisters.

The next day is bid day and Tri-Delt invites me to join! I'm given tons of stuff with Tri-Delt written all over it, including a Tri-Delt T-shirt that I'm instructed to change into immediately for the hourlong photo session, the proofs of which will surely be featured in future slide shows. Then I go to dinner with all my new sisters at Planet Hollywood in Beverly Hills where the sisters seem to relish my stories about other sororities. "What were the other houses' skits like?" they ask. After dinner, Laura and two other sisters drive me back to campus. When they ask where they can drop me off I gesture to a dorm, get out, blow good-bye kisses, wait until their taillights disappear, and scurry back to my motel.

Because bid night is still an official sorority event, no alcohol is allowed, which means there's no drinking during rush until . . .

Saturday. At eleven a.m I get on a fraternity beer bus (so called because there's an active keg and lots of drinking on board) with my sorority sisters and we go to the Rose Bowl where we watch a football game. Watching a football game really means hanging out and watching all the other rushees to see who's joined what sorority, which determines what boys they'll be introduced to. A Rho Chi who can now reveal her Tri-Delt ties informs me that out of the 430 rushees who started rush, only 260 survived. I think of what I would have done had I not gotten into Tri-Delt. I would have had to switch schools I conclude—an odd thought considering I'm not even enrolled. But the desire to belong, the desire to be accepted during rush is that infectious. Through the crowd turnstiling into the stadium, I see Deborah Who Likes Doritos with her mother. I look away before she can see me.

Saturday night there's a party for the new pledges. Because sororities can't have parties, on Saturday night each of the sororities goes to a party at the fraternity they associate with—i.e, the house most of the girls have boyfriends in—so Phi Psi hosts Saturday's soiree. As far as I can tell, like the skits that are passed down from year to year, the fraternity affiliation is something of an heirloom as well. The older members of a sorority may associate with a particular fraternity and then the new rushees meet boys from that fraternity and thus the trend continues.

The party takes place in what are actually three apartments joined by an outdoor stairway. This floor plan plays an essential part in the trafficking of desire: Girls and boys walk up and down the stairs, and up and down again, the boys in search of beer, the girls hoping to bump into the fraternity boy they're interested in. The incentive to climb the stairs (aside from the hope that you'll run into whoever's playing the Rochester to your Jane Eyre) is that on the balcony of the top floor is a keg. On the second floor is a bar with hard alcohol, and stacked up on the bar are plastic pledge cups—24 oz. cups on which each of our names and three triangles have been painted with bright colors. I get my cup and strike up a conversation with a lanky, black Phi Psi pledge about how he decided on Phi Psi.

"I hung out there one of the first nights I was down here [L.A.] and I liked the guys so I kept hanging out with them and I said I wanted to pledge."

"That's it?" I say. I can't believe he's forgone the scantron, the blisters, the tears, the dressing up, the dance performances, the starvation, the lemon water, the revivals of *Dick Tracy* and *Grease*. "Yeah." He shrugs. "Why, what did you have to do?"

" . . . "

This is not to say that joining a fraternity is easier than joining a sorority, but rather that the emphasis on rushing versus pledging differs. For sororities, it's getting chosen during rush that's the hard part. During the subsequent nine weeks of pledging, pledges get showered with presents, like candy, and their most grueling tasks entail bringing the sorority sisters slurpies at three in the morning. Suddenly food is allowed—if only as a gesture of affection, one that is acknowledged without necessarily being consumed. Pledges also have to learn factoids about the sorority, such as where the first chapter was located and the year it was founded. At the end of pledge period, the pledges dress in white dresses and go through a ceremony called Presents, in which there are (more) dance performances and skits and the pledges are presented as sorority sisters.

In contrast, joining a fraternity follows the opposite course. After extensive partying during rush week, fraternity pledges set off on an *Iliad*-like series of hardships that they must endure while pledging. This disparity reflects the difference in the focuses of fraternities and sororities as well: Sororities concentrate on appearances, as evidenced by rush; fraternities on the extended bonding that occurs during the grueling trials of the pledging period.

I think about the differences between fraternities and sororities and how boys join fraternities primarily for the male bonding and the beer, whereas girls join sororities for sisterhood and the fraternity boys. What beer is to fraternity boys, popularity among fraternity boys is to sorority girls. Having had this epiphany, I make my way to where the boys are—the keg. There, I spot another Tri-Delt pledge. I don't know her name, but she hugs me hello—after all, we've both been preapproved by Tri-Delt, and together, we wait to be served.

The scene at the keg is this: The fraternity boys are acting like fraternity boys and the sorority girls are acting like sorority girls in a fraternity boy's fantasy. At one point, the Keg Master informs the keg groupies—Tri-Delt sisters and others—"Okay, we're going to serve the girl wearing the lowest-cut shirt first."

I'm unprepared for the response Keg Master gets. All the girls, except for me and my fellow neglected narrow-faced pledge, pull down the necklines of their shirts so far that the lace of their Victoria's Secret bras shows, and they even pull that down a bit, too. The scrawny Keg Master and his beer-bellied second in command ascertain which of the low-cut shirts is the lowest (that of a busty beauty who's exposing the roseate tip of her right nipple), and thereby establish a pecking order.

When the Keg Master has worked his way down the hierarchy determined by largest amount of exposed breast, he resumes pouring beer for his friends. At last, he spots my still-empty pledge glass. "Oh my God," he says. "Why didn't you tell us who you were?"

"Excuse me?" My heart races as quickly as my thoughts. They know I'm not Katie Wintersen, they all know. What the hell am I going to do now? I won't even be able to get away given that I am on the top floor of this crowded party.

"I mean," he continues, "why didn't you tell us you were a Tri-Delt? We would have had you a beer in no time." He takes my cup and plants the nozzle inside and I look at the name Katie that's been painted on the cup in big, aqua blue letters. I realize how comfortable it was to slip into Katie Wintersen's identity, how by simply taking on that identity I suddenly had a social life—friends, parties to go to, boys to fill my cup with beer.

As the beer foams to the top of my cup, the backward baseball-cap wearing Keg Master spews out some fraternity lingo: "Now you're golden," he says, which, translated, means that as of now, I'm all set. I sip my beer and think about how for a lot of these girls, taking on the identity of a sorority, just as I took on that of Katie Wintersen, offers them the same sort of reassurance. Once they've gone through rush, they too, are deemed golden.

A few days later, I go back to New York because classes have started and transcripts are being sent to the houses, and lists of rushees are being delivered to the Pan-Hellenic office, and I sense that the discovery of my nonenrollment/nonexistent status is only a few computer entries away. I tell Laura the reason I'm leaving L.A. and going back home is because of an emergency situation with that ex-boyfriend I told her about. Lying to Laura is terrible for two reasons. She's a nice girl (after all, she preffed Katie). Plus, I feel that my journalistic endeavors have deprived Laura of having a younger sister and I've deprived someone else of having her as a silver sister. And who knows what might have happened to that little sister whose place I appropriated? She may have brought in a little sister, who would grow up and write letters of recommendation for would-be Tri-Delts who would grow up and write recommendations, etc. In short, I've fucked with evolution.

I go back to New York with all the paraphernalia of membership: a Tri-Delt T-shirt, water bottle, pencil, and a pewter key chain with three triangles. I also go back with something less tangible: a new understanding of the appeal and advantages of group membership. I realize that sororities provide college arrivistes with a perfect blend of freedom and security; sororities, like many American organizations, offer their members a new social identity, but one that has the solidity and widespread recognition that comes with age. I walk down the streets of the East Village, where I live, and like a girl with a new haircut, I feel that everyone can notice something about me has changed.

But my friends don't notice much. They ask about rush—they call it ridiculous and superficial and at the same time my male friends ask to see photographs of my new sisters. But my friends in New York are different from my sorority sisters. Unlike the Tri-Delts, my friends don't tell me how much they love me and how special I am to them—these are friends I've had for years and they never tell me. They don't decorate cups with my name for me to take to parties, and sometimes they even grab a drink right out of my hand. What do I have in common with these people anyway, I wonder. Maybe it's just a coincidence that all of us who went to grad school together, worked at literary magazines together, and spent our days writing apart all live in the same neighborhood.

But then something happens. The writer friend of mine who was happy I was "screwing over" sorority sisters is annoyed with me for having been won over to thinking sororities aren't all that bad, but his real contempt is directed toward a woman he went to college with who became an investment banker with low-brow taste in art, movies, and literature. It isn't her having low-brow taste as an I-banker he has contempt for, it's that now she's quit her job and published a trashy, low-brow book, and given that she is now ostensibly a writer like him and others could now conceivably believe that, by association, he is a writer of trashy, low-brow works, he's left with no choice but to disown her as a friend. All of his friends disown her as a friend, even those of us who weren't friendly with her. The strength of this reaction is determined by the extent of the previous relationship—the closer we were to her, the more we disown her. And the more we collectively disown her, the closer we all become. She clarifies our definitions of ourselves . . . not unlike the demarcations sororities make among themselves.

I call Laura after Presents because, frankly, I miss her. She tells me how much she loves me, how much everyone at Tri-Delt loves me. "If you decide to come back to L.A., I'd be psyched to hang out," Laura says. "Seriously, Katie, I mean it, I want to be friends with you forever," she says—and here she pauses, and gulps, and swallows, and takes a sip of something, and then another sip, and says graciously what we both know is a lie—"even if you decide not to be a Tri-Delt."

Laura's sorority affiliation is the cornerstone of her collegiate identity. It determines who she'll be friends with, who she'll date, and even influences her major. To her, the differences between herself and Kappa Kappa Gammas and Pi Beta Phis are both substantive and pronounced. And while the variation among sororities may seem trivial to you, dear reader, perhaps you have more invested in some of these divides: Democrat/Republican, Bulls' fan/Knicks' fan, city dweller/suburbanite, Harvard/Yale, East coast/West coast, Gap-shopper/non-Gap shopper, John Updike reader/John Grisham reader, cats/dogs. Are these distinctions any less arbitrary than those that are made during that intense week of frenetic socializing and fierce scrutiny, that microcosm for the making of Americans, that rush?

CHAPTER TWO

Bikinis & Tiaras: Quinceañeras

With a Giotto blue ceiling sprinkled with gold stars, gargoyles (the only ones I've seen both indoors and with wholly intact ears), and two fountain-sized cages in which colorful birds chirp along to Vivaldi's "Four Seasons" and pick at artfully prepared plates of lettuce and fresh fruit, the lobby of the Biltmore Hotel in Miami, Florida, has clearly been designed to scream "luxury." Three times a day—ten, noon, and two o'clock—use of the space is rented out for $175 to brides and *quinceañeras* who want to have a room—or rather, an opulent backdrop—of their own.

It's one of my first days in Miami and I've come to the Biltmore to observe the noon photo session because that's when fifteen-year old Monica is scheduled to pose for her *quinceañera* (*Keen-se-an-yeh-ra*) photographs. The *quinceañera*, or *quince* (*keen-*say) as it's commonly referred to in America, is the coming-of-age ritual for Latin American girls that transforms them from *niñas* to *señoritas* when they're fifteen years old—*quince años*. In fact, many girls simply refer to the ritual as "having their fifteens." The reason I'm down in Miami, a hotbed of *quince* activity, is to learn more about the current state of the ritual in America.

Although the *quince* is often considered akin to the debutante ball, there are some substantial differences between the two fêtes: Unlike the debutante ball, in which upper-middle-to upper-class girls are presented to society, *quinceañeras* can be of any class (tales of cars being sold and second mortgages taken out on homes to cover the cost of a *quince* are not uncommon), and while the debutante ball is usually held in honor of a group of girls, the *quince* party is typically thrown for one girl, who, as symbolized by her tiara, is queen for the day.

In addition to the requisite tiara, for her photo session today Monica is sporting a cotton-candy pink dress. The dress has six layers of organza ruffles that drape out around her like a multi-tiered cake. A heavyset woman who's wearing blue jeans and red high heels, Monica's mother issues stage directions to both Monica, her sister, and the photographer. "Have her stand over there," she commands. "Would you mind moving over there?" the sister says to hotel guests sitting in couches that could conceivably edge their way into a photograph's border. *"Gracias. Muchas gracias."*

The *quinceañera* holds a rose in her gloved right hand and leans against a piano she doesn't know how to play. Next, she stands beside a gargoyle, her non-rose-holding hand resting on its head as though it's a child, or a dog. Some photos are meant to showcase the back of her dress, with its elaborate stitching and beading, and for these, Monica glances back at the camera over the puff of her leg-of-mutton sleeve.

All this is merely preparation for an even more impressive backdrop. For about half an hour Monica's mother has been eyeing the window that a large party of hotel guests has been congregated in front of, lounging and drinking. When they finally disperse, Monica's mother wobbles over to the window and stands there territorially, the way someone might save a parking space. Monica takes her position in front of a curtain held back with a wide sash and looks wistfully out a window she's never looked out before. The window affords her, and more important, the camera, a view of the hotel's manicured grounds—complete with fountains—and beyond, the upscale neighborhood of Coral Gables.

Like mannequin dressers in a department store, Monica's mother and sister tend to her. Her mother pushes back her shoulders to fix her posture and secures one of Monica's curling-ironed ringlets behind the tiara. Backing away, so as not to miss the spectacle for a moment, she smiles exaggeratedly at her daughter, the way mothers smile at babies whose pictures are being taken, hoping that this will encourage them to smile back.

The photographer glances at the mother and she nods and then holds her hands together, as though in prayer. "Smile," the photographer says to Monica. "You're not always going to be fifteen."

From the way Monica is dressed and the way her mother and sister are acting, I'm sure that she is headed off for the biggest party of her fifteen-year life. So when the photo session is over, I ask Monica where the *quince* festivities will be held.

Wearing perfume that smells like hibiscus, she smiles an equally sweet smile and says, "I decided not to have a party. Instead, my mom and I agreed that for my fifteens I would have my pictures."

This is it, she is telling me, and this, I think, is bizarre.

After a few more days in Miami I learn that increasingly, many Cuban girls who turn fifteen forego the ritual of the *quince* altogether and instead, like Monica, opt for what is known as "having your pictures." This isn't because the *quince* parties are any less popular than they used to be, but rather the opposite, because *quince* parties have become so important and elaborate and costly and competitive, many lower-to middle-class families in Miami today opt to devote all their time and effort to the end result: the photos.

No one knows the precise origins of the *quince*—some say it dates back to the Aztecs and Mayans. Michele Salcedo, author of *Quinceañera!: The Essential Guide to Planning the Perfect Sweet Fifteen*

Celebration writes that the Duchess of Alba, in eighteenth-century Spain, is credited with starting the custom.

> The duchess would invite girls on the cusp of womanhood to the palace and dress them up as adults for the first time. Similarly, although a century later, the Empress Carlota of Mexico invited the daughters of the members of her court to be presented as young ladies eligible for marriage. In both cases, there would be a party, with a feast and the dancing of intricate figures, as was the custom of the time, a custom that is carried over to the *quinceañera* celebration today.

Whatever its origins, in most Latin American cultures when a girl celebrates her *quince* she has a church ceremony, followed by a reception at which she has a court of fourteen couples, one representing each year of her life. Once the *quinceañera* has made her entrance in her simple white gown and her father has crowned her head with a tiara, removed her flat shoes, and fitted her feet with high heels, and she has waltzed with him, then boys her age, and finally, with her escort, her *chambelán de honor*, it is finally understood that she is now an adult. What being an adult in *quince* terms means is that as of the day of the ritual, the young woman is allowed to start wearing makeup, high heels, and more revealing clothing; shaving her legs; going to parties; and dating men.

But much of this simplicity and tradition is a thing of the past.

"*Quinces* are all different now," says Angela Lopez, a fifty-year old Miami woman who went through her *quince* in Havana, Cuba, before her family moved to America. "It used to be the *experience* of the day of your *quince* that was important," she says. "My parents kept me at home all the time before I turned fifteen. My *quince* was a ritual that said I was allowed to start going out and be seen. I was allowed to start painting my lips and wear makeup in public."

"*Quince* parties today have turned into carnival theme shows with women in Marie Antoinette dresses pulling elaborate stunts," concurs Dulce Goldenberg, a teacher at Miami High who went through her own *quince* in Cuba and is now regularly invited to her students' *quinces* in Miami. "I've been to *quinces* where the girls even make their entrance in a hot air balloon." She shakes her head. "Hot air balloons!"

These days the presentations compete to be more inventive and expensive than the *quince* the guests attended only the week before. This is especially the case in Miami, where most of the young *quinceañera*'s families are from Cuba. Salcedo, author of *Quinceañera!*, told me that in her research of *quince* parties across the country she found that Cubans in Miami often went to much greater, more elaborate and costly lengths for *quinces* than other Latinas celebrating their *quinces* in, say, San Antonio or Chicago.

"A lot of Cuban mothers who wanted to have *quinces* when they were young never got the chance to [because of the political situation]," Salcedo told me. "When they left Cuba, they left with nothing. When they came to America, however, a lot of them became successful, and their daughter's *quince* has become an important way of showing their friends and family that they've made it. While Mexican Americans in Texas might celebrate a *quince* with a rented dress and a five-dollar-per-person barbecue plate, Cubans in Miami buy the dress and even middle-class families can spend $100,000 a pop on the parties."

In Miami today, it's not uncommon for the *quinceañera* to make a formidable entrance to her party that entails, yes, a hot air balloon, a Cinderella-like horse-drawn carriage, a spinning carousel on which she sits side-saddle on a horse, or a large seashell that whirls around electronically and from which the *quinceañera* emerges like Botticelli's Venus. In fact, in some of the photos I've seen, the *quinceañera* is almost as scantily dressed as the Renaissance beauty: Posing in a bikini, her legs shaved, her lips red, she smiles seductively, as if to advertise her new status as a *señorita*/Lolita.

· · ·

Of course, the extravagance of *quinces* exists all around the country, and so do its critics—many of whom are church officials and educators. Although, unlike the bat mitzvah, the *quince* doesn't have a particular religious significance, many families choose to have a private mass for their daughters on the day of the party so they can thank God for bringing them into the world. But many in the Catholic community feel that this is not enough, that the dress often becomes more important than God, and that the ritual—not to mention the photographs of bikini-clad poses—can emphasize a girl's sexuality. Addressing these concerns, in the past ten years many archdioceses, such as the archdioceses of Phoenix, Arizona, Los Angeles, California, and San Antonio, Texas, have begun issuing guidelines. The guidelines vary, but they can include advising that girls take five classes of Bible study, Hispanic history, *quince* history, and modern morals, and that the girls go on a church-sponsored retreat with their parents before the event.

After Father Antonio Sotelo, a vicar for Hispanic affairs and a pastor at Immaculate Heart in Phoenix, Arizona, circulated his guidelines around the diocese, several churches, including Immaculate Heart, started sponsoring *quince* classes and retreats. When I call Father Sotelo to ask what he thinks of *quinceañeras* who opt not to include a mass in their *quince* celebration, he bluntly tells me, "That's not a *quince*, that's just a party. The mass shows their special relationship to the Lord, to the community, to their parents."

"Do you think people should have to have masses as part of their *quinces*?" I ask.

"Well, it's a free country," he says. Despite his words, there's disapproval in his voice. Then his tone changes as he adds, "But all the girls who come here to Immaculate Heart are really committed to the *quince* mass. We have them write letters saying why they want to be a *quinceañera* and some of the letters are so personal you can hardly read them. In the letters they thank the Lord for their families and, if they've been fighting with their families they talk about how they want to start getting along, they talk about mistakes they've made, how they want to renew their baptismal vows, about how they miss their grandparents who have died.

"The girls are all so *sincere* in what they say," Father Sotelo continues. As his enthusiasm and praise for these young women increases, so does the speed with which he speaks. "People say the wild years are twelve, thirteen, fourteen years old. I think the wild years are eighteen and up. Some of the young brides who come to me to get married are spoiled brats. At least with the *quinceañeras* they mean what they say. I'd rather do ten *quinces* than one wedding. I could do *quinces* all day long."

One person in the Catholic Church who makes it her crusade, as she calls it, to educate and assist parents with their preparation of the *quince* is Sister Angela Erevia. Sister Angela, who has written a book about *quinces* entitled *Quince Años: Celebrating a Tradition*, travels around the country leading workshops that encourage parents of all religions and nationalities to plan at least one coming-of-age celebration for their daughters *and* their sons. In fact, she calls the *quinceañera*, the *quince años*, because she suggests young men go through a ritual at age fifteen as well.

When I ask Sister Angela what she thinks about the amount of money families put into their children's *quinces*, she says, "There's not a right way or a wrong way to celebrate. I don't tell people how much to spend on their weddings, so I don't tell them how much to spend on their child's *quince años*. But," she adds, "it doesn't have to cost a lot. In Dallas I helped the diocese organize a *quince años* for seventy-five teenagers and it only cost twenty dollars per family."

"Five hundred years ago in pre-Christian times in Mexico, kids went through ordeals to test their maturity and if they were successful they were considered mature members of their community," Sister Angela says to me during a phone conversation. Her voice is patient yet firm and I can't help but envision her as a Hispanic Julie Andrews in a modern adaptation of *The Sound of Music*. "Today we don't have to put our kids through ordeals. There is already so much pressure in the environment, with alcohol, divorce, suicide, premarital sex, teenage pregnancy, and there's nothing that affirms teenagers' presence."

In her workshops Sister Angela encourages parents to use the *quince años* to help their children understand who they are and where they come from. "It's an opportunity to develop their identity," she says.

Esther Nodarse who, with her husband, Aurelio, runs a successful party planning service in Miami called Pretty Party, says that she's seen a change in the *quince* in the twenty-five years since she started her company. It used to be that girls born in the U.S. thought the *quince* was "a tacky, Cuban tradition, and they wanted to be more American than Cuban and celebrate their sweet sixteen." But today, she says, many of the girls encourage their parents to have *quinces*, and therefore in Miami it's becoming more popular than ever before. She estimates that nowadays about 90 percent of Cuban girls have some sort of celebration.

I spent some time at Miami High, talking to girls about the *quince* to find out what it meant to them. Miami High is an inner-city high school with a primarily Latino student body. It's not famous for much except that *Porky's* was filmed there. No one really knows for sure if the peephole still exists in the boys' locker room; many of the students haven't seen *Porky's*, they just know that an American movie was filmed at their school.

"I'm having my fifteens next month," says one sophomore in a pink halter top and denim miniskirt that exposes cheerleading-toned thighs. All the other girls in the room—those who have yet to have their fifteens, and especially those who have had their fifteens—ooh and ahh as though this weren't something they all went through.

But while these young women believe that getting their driver's license, or graduating high school, or even turning sixteen will all be significant transition points in their future lives, they don't pretend that turning fifteen is in and of itself transformative, because it doesn't give them any new sought-after independence.

So if it's not a big day in that it grants them license to wear makeup, or shave their legs, or date boys—most Miami High students have been doing all of the above for years—then why do they make such a big deal about their fifteens? One reason is that they have inherited their mothers' love for *quinces*. (This is where the oohing and ahhing comes from.) Their mothers are the ones with the memories and the stories of their *quinces* or the regret at not having had one, and they are the ones with the dreams of their daughters' celebrations, and their daughters are born into these dreams. As one young woman with manicured red nails tells me, "I wasn't even born yet and my mother was already saying 'I can't wait for her to have her fifteens.' "

Just as they don't pretend that it means anything more to them than that they're fifteen, these young women don't pretend they go through their *quince* for the sake of tradition. As one young Cuban girl wearing a tight T-shirt with a Betty Boop decal says, "Your parents want it to be as important to you as it is to them, but it's not. Like, we want it because of the party, and they want it because of tradition so their friends will be 'Oh, wow.' To us, it's just a party."

"Yeah," says another, "Having my fifteens wasn't a turning point. It was just a way to celebrate."

A well-groomed young woman who has charm bracelets from both her *quince* and her sweet sixteen, explains why she wanted to have a party, even though her parents offered her a car or a cruise instead, simply to avoid the hassle: "I like to party, and I like being the center of attraction."

The prospect of being the center of attraction is one of the most appealing aspects of the *quince* for these girls. For a day, they get to have their photographs taken by professionals who specialize in child models. For a day, they get to pose in bikinis as though for a fashion spread in *Seventeen* magazine. For a day, they get to wear ball gowns and tiaras and hold roses and when the camera snaps they look like they have just been crowned Miss America.

Even those who are at first reluctant usually enjoy their night in the spotlight. "I didn't want to have a *quince*, because I'm a liberal kind of girl," says Juanita, a sixteen-year-old of Colombian descent who lives in New Jersey. "I always thought that the *quince* was a way for people to say, 'Look at how pretty my daughter is. Look how much money I have. Don't you want to marry my daughter?' When I was fourteen, my mother asked me if I wanted to have one, and I told her 'Look, we're living comfortable, why waste the money?' and I though she would leave it at that."

But Juanita's mother, Yolanda, who had four hundred people to her own *quince* in Colombia, did not leave it at that. For her daughter's sixteenth birthday, she threw her a combination surprise birthday party and *quince* because she wanted to keep up the tradition and also, she said, "It was more to have the pictures to send back home."

I went to the party, held at a banquet hall in Union City, New Jersey, complete with disco ball, a DJ who spun salsa, and figurines of Venus de Milo. There I saw an unsuspecting but happily surprised Juanita greeted with a chorus of "Surprise!" and colorful ribbons thrown in her direction before she was ushered off to the ladies' room to be changed by her mother into clothing fit for a *quince-añera*—a white gown, long white gloves, and slippers. (Yolanda took Juanita's measurements for the dress a few weeks earlier, under the guise of saying, "Juanita, you look like you've lost weight. Let me take your measurements so we can have a record.") When Juanita reentered the banquet hall, Yolanda stalled the start of the ceremony so she could load her camera with film (an oversight in all the excitement) and instructed the guests to make sure to give her their negatives so she could send the pictures to *her* mother, and then the ritual commenced.

Because Juanita's father left when she was three months old, his duties were fulfilled by a cousin who changed her slippers into size 8 white high heels (her mother tried them on Juanita, a heavy sleeper, in the middle of the night to make sure they fit) and crowned her curly-haired head with a tiara. All the while, Juanita held a rose in her gloved hand and sat upright in a wicker chair decorated with pink bows that had been placed in the middle of the banquet hall. "The chair is her temporary throne," her mother explained to me. "Tonight she is queen, but tomorrow she will be a regular person again."

After her shoes had been changed her mother made a toast: "I am toasting the birthday girl because I have been a mother and a father. Juanita, we are here to toast your future because you are starting a new future that's going to be harder." Then she danced the *quinceañera* waltz with her daughter—traditionally reserved for the father—and there were tears in her eyes and tears in Juanita's eyes and tears in *my* eyes. At the end of the waltz, Juanita spun her mother around because even at that moment, she knew the ritual was more about her mother than her.

I spoke with Juanita the day after the party, and she said she now understood why the *quince* tradition was alive. While it made her want to celebrate her own daughter's sweet sixteen, however, she maintained that she won't incorporate elements of the *quince* into her daughter's party. "I think the *quince* is sort of a lost tradition among the second generation," she explained.

"For my fifteens I had my pictures," says a young Cuban woman named Rosa. When I ask her why she thinks young women are increasingly having their pictures taken in lieu of a party she says, "So we can have a memory. We could have a party but we can't, like, keep that to show our children. But if we have the pictures we can show our children, our grandchildren, and they can see, like, our favorite age."

Rosa is a nice girl but she hardly strikes me as having an easy time as a teenager. She complains that she's never been asked out by a boy and she suffers some standard teenage afflictions like being overweight, having a poor complexion, and wearing heavy glasses.

Is fifteen *really* your favorite age? I ask.

She gives me a winsome smile and answers, "You're only young once."

I am sitting in the courtyard of Miami High during a recess with Rosa and Melissa, a petite seventeen-year-old beauty with aqua eyes who also opted to just "have her pictures" for her fifteens. Unlike Rosa, Melissa has had an easy time making friends at Miami High, an easy time being a teenager. While Melissa's role model is Gloria Estefan, Rosa loves the Colorado Rockies, and she's wearing a jacket with their name across the back. The black jacket is much too hot for the Miami sun, but Rosa will do anything to show her loyalty to the team. Melissa's wearing a spaghetti-strapped sundress. What's striking is that both these girls—one thin, one fat, one popular, one with few friends—are prematurely nostalgic about the fifteenth year of their life that *quince* photographs capture.

"The day of your pictures is just the best," gushes Melissa. "It's the biggest rush and everything. Everyone's pampering you and everybody's helping you get dressed and the photographer's super nice and he's saying 'Look here' and 'Do this' and you feel like a model."

"Yeah," chimes in Rosa, "you feel like a model. For the one day you look beautiful—you're like, yeah, I know it, it's cool. You want to see some pictures?"

Before I respond Rosa pulls out a photo album from her backpack. The photo album says "*Mis Quince Años*" on the front and a gold-encircled peephole features her favorite picture. It's a little like looking though the peephole in *Porky's* because there is something prurient about the way Rosa has been made up. She's wearing a low-cut white dress and smiling seductively, leaning against a column that looks like it could be part of a costly mansion but isn't (it's just a solitary column in Coral Gables that doesn't support anything; it is, however, a popular spot for many photo shoots of *quinceañeras*).

The first page of the album is designed for filling in the details of the party; it has spaces in which the names of all the fourteen couples who make up the *quinceañera*'s court of honor are to be written. Since Rosa didn't have a party, this page is blank, as it is in the photo albums of all the other young Latinas who increasingly decide just to "have their pictures." In the back of her album are pictures of other girls' photo sessions. Students at Miami High exchange *quince* photos the way schoolgirls trade stickers. The other photos show the *quinceañeras* posing in front of fake backgrounds, blown-up photographs of waterfalls, white sand beaches, castles. Some even have magazine-like headings embossed on top: "Get attention"; "Looking good"; "Super body."

One of the photos in Rosa's album is of her sister with the president of a club she was trying to get into. "They took pictures and everything, but they didn't end up letting my sister in," Rosa says accusingly, as though they did something deceitful. "My father bought the pictures anyway."

There's something sad about this but not unexpected. This is, after all, a place and an environment where pictures mean more than the truth, where a day in a young women's life is special because photographs are taken of her in various poses.

Of course, photographs from a young woman's fifteens aren't just collected in her album and wallet and those of her friends, they're sent to all the family's friends and relatives. Rosa sent some of the photographs to her grandmother and her parents' friends in Cuba. She says that she saw some of the photographs from girls' fifteens that were taken "over there" (Cuba) and that "the color was faded and the dress wasn't so pretty and the hotel where the pictures were taken was a cheap motel, a roach motel."

For Rosa and others who see the difference between *quince* pictures taken in Miami and their parents' homelands, that is really the issue—the difference in the quality of the photographs and the difference in their dresses. To these girls' parents, however, the difference is that between two worlds, and two social classes. Their parents send the photographs to all their friends in the countries they have left behind as though they were Hallmark cards. This is America—America!—these photographs say, and we have made it.

CHAPTER THREE

Dipping: Debutantes

CRASHING

When you turn onto River Oaks Boulevard, the street that leads to Houston's River Oaks Country Club, and you first lay eyes on the club, your initial reaction might be like mine: Whoa! Even from five long Texas blocks away I see the country club's gate and behind that, its fountain, and behind that, on top of a rise, its multi-columned facade. The club's architecture is like that of a capitol building—which seems appropriate when you consider that it is the social capitol of the exclusive residential area of River Oaks.

It's December and I'm not wearing a coat because this is Houston and it's still sweetly warm out in the early evening and I hold my sleeveless arm out the passenger-side window to feel the air. My tuxedo-clad escort for the evening speeds down River Oaks Boulevard and we pass oak tree after oak tree, their trunks illuminated with white, spiralling Christmas lights that dangle as casually as tennis bracelets as if to emphasize that yes, we have entered River Oaks, home to hundreds of mansions and swimming pools and Houston's wealthy. The entranceways to the mansions usually have only one step up between horseshoe-shaped driveway and front door, and in comparison, the River Oaks Country Club's stairs seem especially impressive: They are steep and white and look like the kind of steps that could have caused Cinderella to lose her glass slipper after the ball.

On the evening of December 22, 1997, 750 men and women, young and old, all dressed in tuxedos or floor-length gowns, climb these steps in their polished black shoes and high heels to watch fifteen young women be presented at the annual River Oaks debutante ball, a tradition that's been going on since the club was founded in 1922. But my friend and I do not go in this way. Instead, given the limited options of the Uninvited—even after I pleaded my case in letter-form to the president of the River Oaks Country Club, I was informed that the debutante ball was for the debutantes and their families and friends—we crash.

My escort, who would like to remain anonymous because he is from Houston and once was a Houston debutante's escort and cares about these sorts of things, has borrowed his parents' Jaguar for the night, and the guards at the gate wave us and all the other fancy cars through. Fortunately, Escort knows the layouts of all of Houston's country clubs—both from summer jobs (coaching tennis; making BLTs) and club-belonging friends—and after parking in a lot by the tennis courts, he takes me in through the staff entrance. Escort leads me through a series of corridors and fern-wallpapered hallways, a labyrinth that rivals that of the Palace of Knossos, until we pass a waiter, who, because we are dressed up, assumes we are lost, and directs us to a staircase that leads us up out of the bowels of the country club. We emerge into the main ballroom, miraculously (to me) having made it past the bell-shaped, ball gowned women who are checking off names on a guest list. Escort gives me a smile that is the black-tie version of a high five. I glance around the main ballroom, which has a fitting decor for the occasion: It is pink with gold trimming and mirrors, a cross between a young girl's bedroom and Versailles.

To come out as a debutante is the ultimate anti-Cinderella story. When a young woman is presented as a debutante, society (in this case, high society) is being told she is of a good family and eligible for marriage. The debutante has no need of a fairy godmother—her family supplies her clothing and transport—and no Prince Charming has to scour the town to find her after the ball—her name is on the "Presentation Ball" program, her parents members of the country club. The age at which a young woman makes her debut is no more than an arbitrary assessment of when a girl is ready for conjugal conjunction. At the River Oaks ball, this is in the winter of a girl's junior year in college.

Debutante balls originated in sixteenth-century England with Queen Elizabeth who supposedly started the custom of formally presenting at court young women who were eligible for marriage. Much of the ritual's current incarnation, however, dates back to the nineteenth century, when Queen Victoria began including the daughters of the Industrial Revolution's increasingly *haute bourgeoisie* along with those of the nobility and gentry. The idea of the presentation of young women to American society started in this country in 1748, when fifty-nine colonial Philadelphia families held Dancing Assemblies, the forerunner to the debutante ball. When America began to prosper during the late 1800s, debutante balls made their way across the Atlantic as a vehicle for wealthy families to introduce their daughters into a class-restricted marriage market.

Elizabeth II ended the British court tradition of debutante balls after the last presentations in March of 1958 because, as Hugh Montgomery-Massingberd writes in *Her Majesty the Queen*, "It was felt that since the war, the ritual of the presentations represented money rather than birth or glamour. An aspiring mama had to do no more than pay a lady who had been herself presented at Court to sponsor her daughter and perform the presentation; her daughter was thereupon on the list and inside the palace. There was not much harm in it. But it was not what the kings and queens had intended."

Though the balls stopped in England, and in America, during the 1960s and 1970s in particular, it was often difficult to gather enough debutantes for presentations in the Northeastern United States, debutante balls have always thrived in the South with its love of lineage and social customs. "Parents get really wrapped up in the tradition of the ball," says Jenene Fertita, one of the chairwomen of the River Oaks ball. "They get really upset if anything changes. People object if the invitations that go out to the ball don't have a gold River Oaks seal on it, because that's what it's been like in the past."

But while most parents of Texas debutantes today say that they want their daughters to be debutantes for the same reason they insist on the gold seals: tradition—because they, the mothers, were debs, and their mothers before them were debs—many harbor a not-so-veiled hope that the ball will ensure their daughters will date and eventually marry someone of their social class.

"I know that the debutante ball is kind of an extension of my parents trying to set me up with guys, and I've always been against that," says Elizabeth, a River Oaks debutante home from Harvard for the holidays and the deb season. She is an unpretentious, blue-eyed brunette whose face exudes warmth without irony. "I hate it, for instance, when my dad says, 'I met a great guy; you need to meet him.' I don't think my parents believe I'm actually going to meet my future husband at the ball, but they do think it's a good way to make connections, and that maybe I'll be introduced to someone through those connections."

According to Elizabeth, who says she was hesitant about coming out because she thought the whole affair was for a bunch of "stuffed shirts," she didn't have much of a choice about whether or not she was a debutante. "My grandmother was a debutante, and so was my mother. My parents actually met at my mother's debutante ball—my father was someone else's escort. I've known since the day I was born that I was going to come out."

This, after all, is a world where girls have grown up going to debutante balls—at River Oaks, the Houston Country Club, Allegro, and the one in Galveston. This is a world where some girls come out at more than one ball. "It all depends on how many country clubs your father belongs to," one debutante tells me.

Multiple coming outs are not uncommon. Many of the River Oaks debs have two presentation balls. Elizabeth came out three times—at Allegro, the all-male club her father belong to; at Assembly, her mother's all-female club; and at River Oaks, because both her parents are members.

"I was invited to come out at the International Ball at the Waldorf Astoria in New York, but my parents wanted me to debut in Texas," says Elizabeth. "I think it was definitely important to them that I come out in Texas because they want me to end up here after school and they want me to marry a Texas guy."

Elizabeth's mother maintains that the reason she wanted her daughter to be presented in Texas is because "it's home." While Elizabeth's mother is much more reserved than her daughter in speech, she's more flamboyant in dress; Elizabeth's ball gown is an elegantly simple strapless white dress, her mother's a sweet cocktail pink with a silver sequined bodice. "The point is to introduce her to my friends and children of my friends," her mother tells me matter-of-factly. "I'm not as interested in having her come out in New York or San Francisco because I don't have that many friends there."

I ask her whether she hopes that by having her daughter come out in Texas, there's a greater likelihood that she will end up marrying and settling down there. "Well, Elizabeth was at boarding school for four years and now she's been at college for three, so there's no telling what she's going to do next," her mother says with a mix of exasperation and admiration for her Daisy Miller of a daughter. "I can't dictate what she does or where she's going to settle down."

Like Elizabeth, most River Oaks debutantes admit that while coming out was their parents' idea, they have fun doing it. "I think the whole debutante ball thing is really prehistoric," one ex-debutante with green eyes and one-karat diamonds in each ear tells me. Both the diamonds and the green-colored contacts were presents from her parents in preparation for her coming out. "But you know, my sisters did it and stuff, and my parents really wanted me to do it, and all my friends were doing it so I was like, Oh, I'll do it, it'll be fun and everything. It's kind of par for the course. Every year there's this presentation and it's really just an excuse for a big party—maybe not for the parents, but for the debs. I mean, my friends and I are so far away from getting married."

Regardless of whether they're close to being ready for marriage or not, on the night of December 22, the fifteen 1997 River Oaks debutantes partake in a ritual that symbolizes that they are. By tonight, all the preparations of a lifetime, with particular emphasis on the preceding several months, have been made. The debutante's parents have made their several thousand dollar contribution to the $65,000 it costs the country club to put on the presentation ball. The amount each family pays depends on how many guests they invite: $100 is the rate per adult guest who's seated at the parents' ten-person table(s) and it costs $50 per "young guest," i.e, friend of the debutante, who sits in the second ballroom, where there's a buffet rather than a sitdown dinner. (A number of the debutantes' friends move into the main ballroom and stand against the wall to watch the presentation.) However, as one debutante's mother tells me, "The main cost of the ball itself is the dress."

Promptly at eight the ritual begins. The president of the club stands behind a podium, stage right, and introduces the debutantes, one at a time. Each of the debutantes has a first name like Kristen or Josephine, names that seem meant to be written in calligraphy, a middle name that is, in most cases, the mother's maiden name, and a last name that is recognizable to most guests from society pages, dinner parties, and golf games.

Wearing a white wedding dress by Victor Costa or Vera Wang, or a dress passed down from her older sister who was also a deb, and with white long-sleeved gloved hands holding a nosegay of light pink flowers that brings out the flush in her cheeks, the debutante walks out on stage and stops where, unseen by the audience, a piece of masking tape is on the stage floor. The president continues in his slow Southern drawl: "Daughter of Dr./Mr. and Mrs.————; granddaughter of the late Governor/Mr. and Mrs.————; Presented by————." From stage right, the presenter, dressed in white tie and tails, makes his entrance. Usually, the presenter is the debutante's father; or, in the case of death or a messy divorce, her brother or stepfather. Whoever he is, he stops at his own masking-taped mark, down stage and to the debutante's right.

When the president has finished announcing the debutante's social c.v., the brass band at the back of the ballroom bursts out with a tune of her choice. The songs range from an orchestral rendition of the Beatles' "Michelle" (to accompany the debut of a debutante named Michelle) to the theme from *Gone With the Wind* to "Deep in the Heart of Texas" (for the ex-governor's granddaughter). And then it's time for the Texas dip.

REBELLION, DEBUTANTE STYLE

Wafting up to the masking-tape-marked spot on the stage floor, each debutante stops, smiles a big smile, and does her Texas dip. No one knows the exact origins of the Texas dip, but it's most likely a regionalized version of the St. James Bow—the bow debutantes did in England when they were presented to the Queen at the St. James' Court. As its name implies, in America, the Texas dip is unique to Texas debutantes. More than anything else, tradition and a propensity for doing things in a grand manner probably inspire Texans to continue the custom while debs in the rest of the country do a simple curtsey. A Texas dip is quite literally a to-the-floor curtsey in which the debutante gets so far down on her high heels that her dress flares out around her like a marshmallow. As the coup de grace, she lays her left ear on her lap for a moment. The reason she turns her head is to prevent getting a lipstick mark on her virginal white dress.

More specifically, she:

(1) begins with her right hand on her presenter's arm and her outstretched left hand holding a nosegay, which is essentially a bouquet on a stick, drops her hands and brings them up together, as though offering flowers to the audience;

(2) with her bouquet in her left hand, extends both arms out to the side of her body, keeping them below her shoulders, bra-line;

(3) circles her right foot behind her, so that if, when her feet are together they're at the 12 o'clock position, her right foot goes to three o'clock, then to six o'clock, and stops behind her at eight o'clock;

(4) squatting very slowly—the slower you go the harder and therefore the more impressive—she goes all the way down and then, when she can go no further sits back on her right leg, and with her left leg in front of her and keeping her back completely flat, she reaches forward with her chin and starts to bend over; at the very last minute she bows her head;

(5) keeping her back flat, she raises it and when her spine is perpendicular to the floor she lifts her head, sighs a breath of relief and smiles.

Of course, each of these steps is supposed to be part of one continuous, fluid motion. One Texas debutante's mother, whose daughter has come out at four balls and will probably come out at at least two more, tells me that when doing the Texas dip, "You're not supposed to be like an elevator jerking and stopping at every floor, but like an escalator going down to the bottom smothly, and then rising back up again."

The point of the Texas dip is to make the debutantes look graceful, like swans. A ballet instructor attends the ball rehearsals to help the debs with their dips, and during the last rehearsal they wear heels rather than flats with their jeans; nonetheless, it quickly becomes apparent that some of the debutantes are more swanlike than others, and that years of practice or strong quadriceps can greatly aid, even rescue, a Texas dip. Upon curtseying all the way to the floor in their heels and their hoops, a third of the debutantes require the help of their presenter's hand to get back to standing position. And even with assistance—or in some cases, rescue—from an extended gloved hand, they wobble and teeter like fawns standing on their legs for the very first time.

After observing several Texas dips at the River Oaks Country Club's 1997 debutante ball, I noticed a pattern: the girls who smile the widest smiles before they curtsey are the ones who can manage the Texas dip gracefully on their own. The debs with the widest smiles are smiling because they know they can do it—they've practiced for months in their sorority houses and in department store dressing rooms, in front of any full-length mirror they came across. The presenters of debs who have perfected a dip are fully aware of their talents as well—they stand removed from the young women, the way a magician might stand far away from a trick in progress to make sure the audience doesn't suspect any sleight of hand.

When done correctly, the debutante looks like a ballerina resting her head on a down pillow, prepared to dream of sugar plum fairies. When done incorrectly, she looks as though drunk and on the verge of passing out, she's doing a nose-dive into a fraternity brother's unmade bed. Regardless of the outcome of the Texas dip, the audience applauds.

Every year there's a girl who refuses to do the dip on the grounds that it's demeaning to women, or simply because she didn't feel it was worth the effort to perfect. This year is no exception. One of the debutantes opts for a simple curtsey, a mere *demi* demi-plie. While the adult guests collectively pause, then clap, hesitantly, the younger guests enthusiastically cheer this rebellion—and in the debutante world, this is Rebellion.

After the more or (sometimes much) less successful dip, her presenter walks her in a circle on the ballroom's square dance floor, his arm through hers. The obvious purpose of this walk is to let the guests get a better view of her dress, of her hair, of her smile, of *her*. Loud whispers bordering on shouts of "She's just the prettiest. Isn't she the prettiest?" can be heard tables away, while rumors of "Her father left the family for a much younger woman" are merely hushed utterances. The debutante smiles and nods at friends; the presenter waves or raises eyebrows at his, and, in a few cases, even gives them a white-gloved thumbs-up.

When all fifteen of the debutantes have come out on stage, curt-seyed, and paraded around the dance floor, they are introduced once again and led on stage by their presenters until all twenty-nine pre-senters and debutantes (one father has two debuting daughters) are on stage. The president announces, "The River Oaks Country Club is privileged to present the 1997 honorees." To the tune of "Thank Heaven for Little Girls," presenters lead the debutantes in a waltz. Photographers' cameras flash as presenters and debutantes strike poses, foregoing a beat for the sake of posterity's picture frames.

With the end of the song comes the moment of meaning. The president says, "Will the escorts please claim their ladies," which sounds to me like an announcement at an airport baggage claim. "Thank Heaven for Little Girls" segues into Cole Porter's "It's De Lovely," the escorts' cue to cut in. This changing of the guards signifies that a young woman who, up until now was her father's daughter, is ready to be some other man's wife.

High school friends or college classmates of the debutantes, the escorts are men from good families. Rarely are the escorts boyfriends. Debutante committees strongly encourage debs not to invite boy-friends to be their escorts because at this age, you never know (the men are asked to be escorts several months before the presenta-tions), and nobody wants last-minute fiascoes, changes in the pro-gram, or tears. In addition, the point of the debutante ball is for debutantes to be introduced to eligible young men, and so for a deb to have an escort she's already involved with would be like bringing one's own food when dining at a four-star restaurant.

When the escorts cut in, it's not the sort of "may I cut in" you see in black-and-white movies, the kind that's accompanied by a tap on the shoulder and a look of surprise on the cut-in-upon man's face. Rather, when the escort approaches, the presenter blithely lets go of the debutante and pats the escort on the back. He turns toward the debutante and opens his arms and she hugs him and gives him a kiss on the cheek. You'd think she was saying good-bye before boarding a plane to Paris for the year, rather than just taking a spin around the dance floor with someone else. But perhaps the debutantes sense that, for their fathers, this is in fact the moment when they are saying adieu to their little girls.

Aside from the escort who's dressed in his Naval Academy uniform, the young men don't look much like your traditional escorts. Some sport ponytails, and despite that afternoon's rehearsal many of them don't know how to waltz. Judging from the way the debutantes hold the men close and comfortably, it is evident that while they may not have been actively partaking in this world of waltzes and balls before tonight, the debs have lived in co-ed dormitories, dated boys, and some, despite what their white dresses are intended to suggest, have had sex.

No matter that the couples bump into each other, that the Naval Academy guy seems overwhelmed (later, her tells me that the debutante ball is "a welcome change of scenery"). No matter that, if anything, the debutantes seem to be leading the escorts. The debutante's dance with her escort says, I am now ready for marriage. Not necessarily with these men, but with anyone else who may be watching (or with the son of any of the adult guests who may be watching).

The day would come, the debutantes' fathers knew, when they would have to let go of their little girls. But even if their daughters aren't close to getting married, at the ball, the fathers seem even less ready for this prospect. Before the escorts' song is over, some of the fathers start cutting in. This time, it *is* the may-I-cut-in move you see in antiquated movies and bad TV shows. Not something that was part of the rehearsal, so the escorts are taken by surprise. They acquiesce, of course, and make their retreat without so much as a good-bye kiss on the cheek from the now-shocked but still smiling—always smiling—debutante. The fathers and the debutantes dance to a medley that includes "All the Things You Are" while, slouch-shouldered, the escorts hang out on the perimeter of the dance floor like sidelined basketball players, waiting to be called back in.

"My husband was so nervous, you'd think it was *his* coming out," one debutante's mother says to another as they sit at adjacent tables, watching their husbands dance with their daughters. Perhaps comforted after this "one last dance" that has affirmed their daughters are still—and may always be—their little girls, the fathers turn them back over to the escorts, and ask the debutantes' mothers to dance. The mothers blush as though it's now *their* coming-out and they move to the dance floor with élan.

Waltzing about the dance floor now are presenters and wives, escorts and debutantes—as if the former were setting examples for the latter: *See, married life can be fun!* When the dance is over, the adults continue dancing to the next song, and the adult guests join them for the one after that, while the debutantes and their escorts seize the opportunity to escape and migrate down a hallway to the other ballroom. This other ballroom is decidedly the "young person's" room; the crowd is comprised of their friends and the band plays rock cover songs.

Unaccustomed to high heels and not wanting to spill their drinks on their dresses, the debutantes lean forward, tilting into conversations, falling into hugs. They dance with escorts, they dance with other girls' escorts. They smile in all directions, especially if there's a camera. They say hello to friends they haven't seen since summer, and to some they haven't seen for years. They receive compliments on their hair, which, more often than not, was coiffed by their mothers' hairdressers. They receive compliments on their dresses, dresses their mothers often dream they will wear on their wedding day as well—which gives you some idea of how imminent the mothers hope this day will be. More soignée than the ebullient white flounces you'd think Southern debutantes would wear, the dresses are short-sleeved or strapless, and many have tiny silk-covered buttons running up the back, three per vertebra.

The topic of conversation among most of the debutantes is the Texas dip—one who did it perfectly claims "it was no big deal." Another, who wobbled as though she had just been at sea, says, "At least I didn't pull an Amanda S.———," and all the debutantes who are gathered together smile in recognition of the name of the deb who fell to the floor the year before.

Inspired by nostalgic chivalry of days gone by, the escorts and the young male guests crowd around the open bar to fetch drinks for the debutantes and their female friends. But the girls here aren't ones to sit around like women in an Edith Wharton novel. They've been to keg parties at fraternities and they forge ahead to get their own drinks. Flashing smiles in lieu of IDs, some of them say to the bartenders, who are frenetically trying to accommodate the crowd, "Could you please make it a double?"

As Dixon Wecter writes in *The Saga of American Society*, "In the mid and later nineteenth century, the medium [of the deb ball] might be an elaborate dance, but more typical was the afternoon reception, at which the debutante received with her mother and father and a few of her best girl friends, greeting not only young men but a liberal assortment of dowagers and old gentlemen. After the crowd had gone, an informal dinner followed, and lastly a dancing or theatre party for her intimates."

At the time Wecter was writing, in the 1930s, he noted that, "With the increasing financial wariness of these times, it is perhaps not surprising to learn from a recent tally made in New York City that only some 30 percent of a season's debutantes now marry within the year, and about 20 percent the following year." With such discouraging returns on their investments, he wrote, many parents were opting for one of several cheaper alternatives, such as simply sending out cards with the daughter's name engraved below that of her mother's.

Times have changed. Not only have balls become the only way to come out—imagine your confusion if today you were to receive the aforementioned engraved card—they have also become more extravagant than ever. But even the balls have taken a backseat to the private parties each debutante's parents throw for her. "During the deb season you can blow ten thousand dollars in a minute," chairwoman Jenene Fertita says, and it is the parties, more than anything else about being a debutante, that flaunt the wealth behind the ball.

The parties usually have themes like the 1920s or New York, New York, or take place in unusual venues. One debutante this year had a party in a Houston parking garage; on every floor there was a different band playing. While some view this extravagance as a sign of the archaic nature of the ball and imagine the parties to be a throwback to a time when it was important to spend a lot, judging by Wecter's chronicles, the inverse is true: Rather than getting less costly as they've become less relevant, coming out has become a more extravagant and expensive undertaking.

Given that it's not uncommon for parents to spend tens of thousands of dollars on their daughter's private party, it's unsurprising that some view these parties as nothing more than "dressed-up dowries." As one young woman at the River Oaks ball who, parentally clubless, wasn't invited to come out, tells me over her buffet plate of egg rolls and diamond-shaped pastries, "The parties are really fun, but I don't know if I believe in what they stand for. I mean, basically they're saying, Don't you want to marry me after seeing how much money I have? Personally, I've always been one for personality."

ESCORT SERVICE

And what of the escorts, these men who don white tie for the night and help make women out of their debutantes—though not (necessarily) in the colloquial sense. "I've got to think how to say this," confides one beer-bellied escort from Houston whose sister made her debut the year before. "So there's a lot of crap involved in deb balls, right? It's so old school, probably there's some racial stuff you could tie into it. But despite the fact that it's so traditional and old and plantation like, at the same time it's a lot of fun," he says, and as he takes the final sip of his strawless mint julep he tries to avoid, with considerable difficulty, getting any mint in his mouth. "You just have to acknowledge that there's a lot of crap involved. I mean, sometimes I'm like, man, I'm not sure if this is what I stand for, like class and stuff, but at the same time, it's a blast."

For the escorts who aren't from Houston, the ritual and riches of the ball can be like something from a foreign country, or something from Texas. "I grew up in D.C. and went to private school, so I didn't think this would be that different a scene," says one escort whose mother made him get a haircut before the ball. "But I have to say that I'm so overwhelmed. I've never seen anything like this." He gestures around the room. "I mean, the expense itself."

Elizabeth's mother, who met her husband at her coming-out, tells me that many of her fellow debutantes met their future husbands at parties during the deb season. "The men we met were other girls' stags," she explains.

But these days it seems the other girls' stags aren't as interested in meeting the debutantes. Two escorts confess to me that between the rehearsal and the deb ball itself, they did call on some ladies . . . at a local strip club. "We had some time to kill because both our debs' last names are in the beginning of the alphabet and so they take those pictures first," the younger looking of the two tells me. "So, we thought, why wait around?" In their tails, they jumped into one guy's car and sought other forms of entertainment.

"I think I'll tell my deb's parents on her wedding day," says the second escort, and licks his lips as though relishing the prospect of it. "That way they'll be relieved I didn't marry their daughter."

A CONFESSION

"Being an escort was the worst experience of my life," confesses one ex-escort. "Watching the too-young-to-be-overly-made-up-and-overly-dressed-up girls curtseying made me want to puke."

"That is," he hastens to explain, "all of them but my date."

This last qualification is only a nicety because, you see, I was the date.

What I'm talking about here is me when I was seventeen, and something I rarely talk about, my coming out as a debutante, albeit California style. My best friend's mother was on the invitation committee and half the girls who had gone to my all-girls' elementary school were invited to come out. Unlike the debutantes in Texas, many of whom told me that for them debuting was something they'd been groomed for from an early age, something they were expected to do ("like piano lessons") and something that, like piano lessons, they would one day be happy they'd endured, my parents didn't even really know what a "debutante" was. There was no country club they belonged to and therefore no club behind the cause—only a hospital charity that they decided donating $1,500 to was a good thing. My mother, after all, is a nurse, and it was sold to her as "a nice way to celebrate your daughter's graduation." Being from Sweden, she didn't know the ritual had anything to do with marriage. And if she did, I don't think she would have asked me to do it: Unlike most mothers I know, mine told me to wait until I was thirty-five to marry. Thirty-five, *at least*.

And so, with my hair still growing out from where I had shaved half of it off (I had a rough adolescence) and with an ex-boyfriend as an escort, I was presented. Being presented at the Pacific Presbyterian Deb Ball was a truly California event; while most balls are a nod to the distant past, the Pacific Presbyterian Ball (Pacific Presbyterian was the name of the hospital the proceeds went to) was started in 1964. This was when debutante balls were practically dying out in all other parts of the country, save the South. This was the year when Free Speech demonstrations opened an era of protest across the bay, at Berkeley.

What did coming out mean to me? It meant a June full of two, sometimes three events in a day—mother-daughter lunches followed by pool parties followed by a ball at a country club with a band playing standard rock covers—that I fit in between my shifts working at a bakery. I was one of the two debs out of thirty not to have even one party. In short, it didn't mean much. Later, I wished I had given it more thought. Not because I thought the money given to charity was a waste, or because the parties weren't in their own way fun, but because it wasn't me. I was inducted into a scene that I would no longer be a part of. I would soon go to school on the other coast, rarely coming back home. For me, it was more of a good-bye than a debut.

In his novel *Already Dead: A California Gothic*, Denis Johnson writes, "We do what we have to to make it all come true." I think he captures California in that sentence and I think he captures something, too, about the Presbyterian Ball. Whereas in most places, the debutante ball is a reminder of connections to the past—in New York, for example, there's the Mayflower Ball, which is held only for descendants of those who came to this country on the May-flower—in California, it seeks to create connections. It's a way for Californians to establish themselves as part of society, because, like my parents, many Californians, almost by definition, are completely rootless. Here I think of Gertrude Stein's ironic line, "What good are roots if you can't take them with you?"

My reemersion in the deb scene while writing this nine years after my experience prompts me to call some women I know from San Francisco who were in my "deb class" and now, postcollege, reside in the city.

One ex-deb I grew up with who now works for a national clothing chain tells me that she's proud of having been a deb. "I still socialize with a lot of the women who were debutantes and come into contact with a lot of them in my job as well. The deb ball also introduced me to a lot of parents who have helped with my career. I don't dwell on the experience, but I think that it was good in terms of keeping a certain social order working. I mean that in the sense that nowadays it has more to do with female friendships than marriage, per se."

But another ex-debutante who works in San Francisco as a high school teacher tells me that she feels it still has a lot to do with marriage. "Originally it was supposed to introduce a girl into society and signal to men that she was ready for marriage. Well, what's so different about that now? There are plenty of families who are pleased their daughters and sons are being introduced to each other and forming friendships. The summer of parties and that winter are an entire summer and winter break that we spend with a certain group of people. The only difference is that the debs aren't getting married right now like they were fifty years ago. The purpose of coming out is still effective in that regard, it's just a bit delayed and not as concretely stated as it was before."

GREAT EXPECTATIONS

The night before the debutante ball Escort takes me to a party given by two former River Oaks debutantes. It's held at one of the hostesses' family's River Oaks mansion. The women at the party—most of them members of this unofficial sorority of ex-debutantes who have all come out in the past ten years—are so friendly that I think I finally understand what is meant by "Southern charm." In part, this is true. But the other reason they're so welcoming to me is something my friend and I hadn't anticipated: They assume I'm his intended, or at least someone he's serious about. This emphasis on couplings is something they've inherited from their parents. I think of their swanlike dips and how some birds mate for life and how the ex-debutantes seem to want to make certain their friends do, too.

Because of their parents, because they were debutantes, I expect these women at the party—most of whom came out eight years ago—to be married, and about half of them are. Here's the catch: They haven't married the guys their parents probably expected them to marry when they came out; they haven't married men who were escorts or sons of their parents' friends, or sons of the friends of their parents' friends. Instead, the former debutantes have married men who, like most of them, are teachers, or men who, like them, are in graduate school. (So much for the notion that debutante balls can be chalked up as financial investments parents make in their daughters' futures.) The escorts have all gone their own ways and the ex-debutantes who have married into their parents' lifestyle cannot even be counted on the fingers of one glove. I wonder if this non-entree into their parents' world is typical of Escort's friends, or typical of all debutantes coming out in Texas today. "I do know a few debs who married and are in the Junior League, but they're the exceptions," one ex-deb, a high school teacher, tells me. One guest at the party who's married a doctor tells me, "I wasn't even asked to be a debutante."

When the hour is late and all the Christmas cookies have been eaten, we move outside. Under a Texas sky that brims above us like a big cowboy hat, the conversation turns to a memory game: "What song was playing when you went on your first car date?" asks a guy in a Gap denim shirt and khakis. We are sitting in a circle of lawn chairs by a Hockneyish swimming pool, and people take turns responding.

"Tainted Love," one guy says.

"That song from Erasure," says the girl to his right.

When it comes to my turn, I admit I have no idea and have to pass. But the woman sitting next to me remembers exactly—Bruce Springsteen's "Born in the USA." I'm stunned by the capacity of everyone's memories and the fact that they had official dates, not to mention "car dates"—a term I've never heard before. But then I remind myself that this is Texas, where adolescence entails dates and cars, and therefore car dates. This seems so circa 1950, so circa the time their parents were dating, but these young women go through debutante balls because their mothers did, because their parents expect them to. Why shouldn't other aspects of their dating rituals emulate their parents' as well?

Back in the house, the ex-debutantes' parents are talking of their "missing children"—that is, their sons who couldn't make tonight's party. "He's escorting Dr. So and So's daughter," one woman says, and sips her scotch on the rocks.

"Oh really," another replies, her eyebrows arched. Obviously, the name makes an impression.

"They're going to Mr. So and So's daughter's deb party," the first mother continues. "Do you know them?"

"Of course," the second mother replies. She turns to her husband and tells him that Dr. So and So's daughter is coming out.

This is a world of "sons of" and "daughters of," a world of pedigrees. The debutante ball gives the illusion of being all about the young woman, but in truth she is merely a player in her parents' ongoing narrative, one that in Texas, unlike in California, was scripted before the debutantes were even born.

As early as an hour after the presentation of the debs at the River Oaks Country Club, it's evident that coming out as a debutante is no longer a passport into the world of dating—not to mention marrying—the sort of men who are escorts, the sort of men who are "the sons" of their parents' friends. In fact, as the night wears on and the music gets louder and the guests more inebriated, many of the escorts have abandoned the debutantes in favor of other female guests. As one escort tells me, his speech slurred, "A lot of the guys use the ball as a chance to come back and scam on girls they haven't seen for years—some even since high school. We've seen the debutantes—they're always out and about." He pulls at his white tie, as though it's restraining him. "It's the other girls—the ones we thought we've never see again—who we're psyched on."

With their hair freeing itself from hairspray and bobby-pinned buns, with slumped shoulders and torn hems, and some even missing their gloves, the debutantes wander to and fro, from the adult ballroom to the kids'. The adult room is where all the tradition takes place, introductions of "this is my daughter" to a young man's parents as the band plays "In the Mood." In the kids' room is where the aforementioned young man (whose parents are being introduced to a debutante) is most likely wooing a nondebutante as they dance to "YMCA" and "Brown Sugar."

By midnight most of the debutantes are leaving the ball. It's not a matter of having to run home before their carriages metamorphose into pumpkins: These girls have limos that will take them to whatever afterparties their hearts desire. Tonight, the big afterparty is at the Velvet Elvis, a dive bar that has spent a great deal of money trying to look like a dive bar. Before heading off to the Velvet Elvis, debutantes change from their white gowns into casual wear, not because they're afraid their dresses will turn to rags, but for the sake of comfort, and because outside the confines of the country club, the whole debutante thing seems a bit embarrassing.

Their mothers don't go to the afterparty, but remain at the ball until the wee hours, drinking and dancing with their husbands, and the fathers of other debutantes, and those of escorts as well. This, after all, is really their party. Before heading off to the Velvet Elvis myself, I go into the women's lounge to see the debs change into casual wear, but none are to be found. Instead, I feel like Pip in *Great Expectations* when he meets Miss Havisham and finds her dressed for her wedding day, cake and all. The Miss Havishams I see, however, aren't women preserved for their wedding day, but two debutantes' mothers acting as though it's *their* night to debut. I watch as the deb mothers study themselves in the mirror, brushing their mascara wands over their already mascaraed eyelashes and lipsticking O-shaped mouths with Chanel red. Having painted her lips, one mother pauses, puckers, and kisses a Kleenex. "Did your daughter enjoy yourself?" she says, addressing the other debutante mother's reflection.

And the second one, who's wearing a debutante-white dress, says, "Oh, yes," and explains. "Tonight I think my daughter finally learned how fun it is to be the center of attention." Through the fabric of her dress she cups her breasts in her palms and pushes them up so that cleavage, albeit oversunned and wrinkled, spills over her low-cut neckline. "I'm happy for her, I really am," she says and stares at her own eyes in the mirror with visible sadness. "I discovered too late in life that I love being the princess."

PART TWO

Going It on Her Own

CHAPTER FOUR

Just Like Family: Gang Girls

GREEK LETTERS AND ROMAN NUMERALS

"You've got to show interest, commitment, and dedication if you want to be a member," says twenty-five-year-old Maria. "You've got to look good—your hair has to be styled, your clothes have to be well ironed and creased. You can't look trashed because if you become a member you're representing an organization and you have to be committed to the organization."

Maria could easily be a sorority sister elaborating on the Greek system's codes of conduct, but she's not. Maria, who grew up in East L.A. and has dark scars the size and shape of salamanders on her back and extending out from the corner of her right eye (both the result of stabbings), is talking about being in a gang.

In many respects, belonging to a gang and belonging to a sorority are quite similar. Just as choosing one sorority over another is often an arbitrary decision based on meeting one member and subsequently getting to know the others, so is joining a gang. Both sororities and girl gangs have a social infrastructure founded on partying and boys, and yet initiations into both groups are treated as anything but trivial: Sorority pledges have to memorize countless historical facts about the house they're joining while gang members subject themselves to being "jumped in," or beaten up by all the girls in the gang. Once initiated, members of both groups flaunt their devotion to their respective organizations through dress—sporting a sweatshirt embossed with the Greek letters of their sorority or wearing their gang's colors—and action—sticking up for their house or gang, and doing whatever is expected of them by their sisters or homegirls.

And yet, there is a world of difference between what sorority sisters and gang girls are expected to do.

While a sorority sister may be asked to help with rush or organizing dad's day, when every father is invited to accompany his daughter and her sorority sisters to a football game, gang girls may be asked to do an armed robbery or kill enemy gang members. Sometimes they do it in the name of their gang without even being asked. This isn't to say that gang girls are necessarily more innately violent or corrupt, but that they have more at stake. While sororities may provide their members with a house and a sense of family away from home, gangs provide their members with the only family and security they know in a dangerous world. They want to make sure that everyone in their gang will go the distance—that is, stick up for them in fights, help them out monetarily, bail them out of trouble—should the need arise. And it often does.

As Maria, whose parents were both sent to jail for dealing drugs when she was fourteen, explains to me, "When your family is not around physically because they're locked up, or they're emotionally not there because of alcoholism or domestic violence, when no institution will take you in, or you're being harassed by the cops, and you're being rejected by society as a whole, the gang gives you everything from food to emotional support. It *becomes* your family."

I meet Maria in her office in Los Angeles where she works with the Hispanic community, educating people about AIDS. Her desk is organized with safe sex slogans and condoms and her desk chair is pumped up high (Maria is barely five feet tall). On her bulletin board, where others in the office have pictures of their families, are pictures of Maria and her boyfriend and her gang members. As Maria talks about her job, I'm struck by her use of the words "dedication" and "commitment to the organization," the same phrases she uses to describe one's obligations to a gang. It comes as little surprise, then, when she tells me that she views having been in a gang as a positive experience.

Alicia is a striking seventeen-year-old of Mexican descent with long, dark, curly hair and large, dislike brown eyes. She wears sweatshirts and Adidas sneakers. From her gold necklace hangs a pendant with a relief figure of the Virgin Mary. The fact that she currently attends a two-classroom school in Northern California with a probation officer sitting in the front office—where a principal would sit in a "normal" high school—might give you some indication that she's encountered some trouble in her life. But if it weren't for the tattoos on her hands, you might never suspect she was in a gang.

Alicia has a black X tattooed below the knuckle of her thumb and a black I below the knuckle of each of her fingers except for her pinkie. Together, the X and the three Is add up to XIII, or thirteen, which is the number for *Surenos*, or southerners. Although Alicia lives in Northern California, she is in a *Sureno* gang because she is Mexican. She doesn't know why thirteen is the number *Surenos* claim as their own (it's because the thirteenth letter of the alphabet is M, which originally stood for Mexican Mafia, a street gang that started in L.A. in the twenties and now operates primarily in the prison system), she just knows that anytime someone rolls a set of dice and they turn up twelve, everyone in her gang yells "thirteen" because they want everything to be thirteen.

Even if gang girls don't know the history of their gangs, they know who their enemies are. It doesn't matter that Mexico is north of Central America and yet Central Americans are usually *Nortenos* (northerners) while Mexicans are *Surenos*, it doesn't even matter if a Mexican becomes a *Norteno*. None of it has all that much to do with geography, nor, increasingly, with nationality—all that matters is that these girls will do anything for whatever gang they choose to join.

It takes almost no provocation for a fight to break out between *Surenos* and *Nortenos*, who claim the number fourteen. (*N* is the fourteenth letter of the alphabet. In addition to claiming different numbers, *Nortenos* and *Surenos* also wear different colors: *Nortenos*, red; *Surenos*, blue.) "Them looking at you funny" or "throwing their signs at you," or a *Sureno* calling a *Norteno* a *chapeta*, or a *Norteno* calling a *Sureno* a *scrap* is reason enough. The fights take place at McDonald's or Baskin Robbins or at the beach or at the intersections of gang terrain. Sometimes the difference between being on one block rather than another can be the difference between life and death. When talking with gang girls, the belief that everything is a life-or-death situation is almost a refrain, in part because to some degree it's true, and in part because they see much of their world in black and white.

Alicia says the reason she and her fellow gang members claim *Sureno* even though they live in the north is because, "We're Mexicans, and it's like we're proud of Mexico, and you know, Mexico's in the south so we claim it 'cause, even though this isn't Mexico, we're representing it. We consider Mexico the south, so we claim it here because that's like showing that we do love our country." Alicia says that fights often break out between *Nortenos* and *Surenos* simply because of what they claim. She cites examples of being on BART (Bay Area Rapid Transportation) with her "homies" and someone will say "What's your claim?" and if the people asking happen to be *Nortenos* and Alicia and her friends say they're *Surenos*, a fight will break out right there. Even if the fight is between her friend and someone else, Alicia says she joins in because "you ain't goin' to see your homie go down, you're going to jump in."

Alicia's hands and forearms are also "tatted down" with homages to love. She has numerous tattoos in honor of her ex-boyfriend—

tattoos she got when they were still going out. His full initials are barely visible now, but she still has a J, which she originally got in honor of him, tattooed on her shoulder. Now that they're broken up, however, she tells people that the J is for her father, because his name starts with a J, as well.

Alicia was raised in a suburb of San Francisco that has one of the highest murder rates in America. She started smoking marijuana in third grade, and most of her memories of that year are of falling asleep in class. In fourth and fifth grade she straightened up a little bit, but then in the sixth grade it was "weed, weed, alcohol, alcohol." Alicia says, "My mom caught me with a bag of weed and was like, 'What is this?' and I was like, 'I don't know,' and since then it was like no trust and then I was like, 'Forget it, then I don't need you, you know. I've got my friends.' "

Alicia's parents made many efforts, including moving to another city, to keep her out of trouble, but the move only proved to exacerbate the situation. After the move, Alicia would tell her parents "I'm going out," and then run back to where her friends were and not come home for three or four months.

It was around this time that Alicia started hanging out with a girl who was a *Sureno* and, eventually, Alicia decided not only to be in a gang, but to start her own. To her, "gang banging," or being in a gang, is more than just hanging out with other people in your gang. Gang banging means that "they're there for you and you're there for them," Alicia says. "It's just like family."

If you give Will Lopez a map of San Mateo County he can point out where all the various gangs are located. He can show you where the main strip of L.M.G. (Little Mexican Gang, *Surenos*) terrain is (14th Street) and where the 18th Street gang (made up of mostly Central American *Nortenos*) kicks it, which, you will see, is not so far from where the primarily Samoan and Tongan Shoreview gang hangs out. His finger will rest on areas with suburban-sounding street names like Palm and Pacific, Grove and Church, Maple and Chestnut as he tells you what he's seen go on between these gangs, and you will believe him because he is a probation officer for the county of San Mateo and he has seen it all.

Will Lopez has seen kids who are beaten so hard when being jumped into their own gang that they end up with severe brain damage. He has heard thirteen-year-old girls who are in gangs say that every night when they go to sleep they thank God they've made it through another day alive. He has seen the shootings with the Uzis or AK-47s that every gang member seems to own these days. He can show you a box full of red and blue bandanas that are often the sole cause of the shootings and that he's confiscated when picking up these kids who believe "We're down for our turf and we're going to die here." He'll tell you that he often has to bring mothers in to see their child's tattooed body before they believe their child is involved in a gang. And he'll tell you how he was almost killed once when a mother snuck a gun in to her son who was in juvenile hall.

He'll tell you that ninety percent of kids involved in gangs come from single-parent families. He'll tell you how girl-gang members these days are especially dangerous because they feel they have to prove that they're "down." He'll tell you other ways that gangs have changed, about how Hispanic gangs in the twenties were all about zoot suits and dressing up, not about killing. He'll tell you how gangs have gotten out of control even since when he was a kid, when he was in a gang. And you will look at him with his dark hair slicked back like a stockbroker's and his flecked tie and gold tie-pin and white shirt (he never wears red or blue because in these parts even wearing a red Stanford sweatshirt can get you killed), and you will almost not believe him.

But this is the truth and this is one of the first things he tells gang members when they're on probation and he's trying to convince them to leave gang life. He tells them how he was forced to join his neighborhood gang because he had to cross a gang-controlled street to get home every day, and he tells them how he was initiated: He was locked into a dark bathroom and beat up. He tells them how his mother never knew he was ever involved in a gang because he led a kind of double life, and how he left gang life because of his love for his mother and with the help of a soccer coach who got him off the streets and onto the soccer field. In his office you can see a poster of him on the San Jose Earthquakes soccer team, the same poster he sometimes points to when he talks to gang members about how he left his gang. After sharing his story with gang members, he tries to encourage them to leave their gangs, too. He tells them to stop wearing their gang's colors and to remove their tattoos, to trust in him because he accepts them no matter what, and that he will be their best friend; he will back them up. He encourages their families to move because the gangs kids get involved in are usually in the neighborhood and the only way for a parent to get his or her kid out of the gang safely and for good is to change neighborhoods.

Will Lopez knows that today, leaving a gang often means risking one's life and the safety of one's family. He knows that today the gang problem is only getting worse—that kids are being recruited at a younger age and that weapons are now almost as numerous as the red and blue bandanas themselves. He knows all the statistics, too; he knows that the Department of Justice estimates there could be as many as 175,000-200,000 criminal street members in California and that by the year 2000 that number could rise to 250,000, with an estimated 135,000 Hispanic gang members, 90,000 African Americans (particularly Crips and Bloods), 20,000 Asian gang members, and 5,000 white ones (with approximately 600 of those being skinheads). He knows the history of various ethnic gangs and knows that the role of the female in gangs has changed with time. He knows that throughout the eighties females had little claim to the gang. They assumed the role of traditional girlfriend and sometimes they were used by male gang members to carry weapons and narcotics because they were less likely to be arrested for gang activities. But nowadays, female gangs, especially Hispanic ones, are starting to evolve exclusive of the traditional male-dominated gangs, and gang girls are participating in drive-by shootings, auto thefts, and assaults to show that they are tough, that they are down for each other, that they are women of the nineties.

DIFFERENT FOR GIRLS

Michelle Zall, who works at a school in Northern California that many former gang girls attend, says that girls who join gangs often come from families where there's a lack of supervision and a lack of things to do outside of the home. They're not involved in school activities and, often, they have low self-esteem. "They're followers," she says.

Girls today who join gangs are often in the same predicament that male gang members were originally in—they were caught between worlds, with no place to call their own. As Gini Sikes writes in her book *8 Ball Chicks:*

The history of gangs is a history of fear—the fear of outsiders. Although their skin was darker, their faith Catholic, Latino gangs grew in Los Angeles for reasons that most street gangs do everywhere, including the white Italian and Irish gangs of Chicago and New York in the mid-1800s and later the German and Jewish gangs—as a result of swift demographic change. In the 1920s, thousands of Mexicans streamed into California to answer the need for cheap labor on farms and desert mines and to find *una vida major*, "a better life". . . . When the Depression hit, Mexicans were no longer needed. Unlike the white immigrant gangs, which eventually disappeared as Italian and Irish youth were absorbed into the larger economy and society, Mexicans remained outcasts, facing more intense discrimination than the most despised white immigrants. California began repatriation, forcing immigrants back across the border.

Throughout the 1930s and 1940s, neighborhood and street gangs formed for protection and identity. Their members were called *cholos*, "people trapped between worlds," originally referring to those on the fringes of indigenous Indian and Spanish colonial cultures in Mexico. In America it meant poor second-generation kids whose parents remained Mexican at heart while their children desired, yet were denied, full American citizenship.

Gangs became havens for those in the fifties and sixties who felt misunderstood and without a home. They also offered something not readily available to those who felt like outsiders: identity and belonging. In the eighties, when girls who had previously just hung out with male gangs started forming auxiliary gangs and even their own gangs independent of males, it was to fulfill these same needs.

Talking with gang girls you hear stories that verge on psychobabble: These girls had fathers who died or parents who divorced and mothers who were always working, struggling to compensate for the lack of a male breadwinner in the family. And yet their stories are also reminiscent of those of earlier gang members. They, too, have nowhere to go. And, many of them, without father figures or role models (not very many of them would count their mothers as role models), turn toward older male gang members for guidance. Of course, some gangs are more boy-oriented than others, some more violent, and some require more commitment, but regardless of its exact nature, the attraction of a gang is the order and family that it provides.

Chapparo, which means "shorty," is fifteen and five one. She was twelve years old and four nine when she first joined her all-girl gang. "My dad died of cancer that year and my mom wasn't really home after that because she was working all the time—all day, every day, except Sunday. My dad had been strict about me being home at a certain time, but after he died I didn't have to worry about that. I started kicking it with the gang more and more. They'd say, There's going to be this party, and there's going to be a crack, and I was a big crackhead so I'd go. I got jumped into a *Sureno* gang and it was really kick back and stuff."

Chapparo is skinny with long brown hair, and like many Latina gang girls, highly arched, extensively plucked eyebrows. She outlines her full lips with dark brown lip pencil and fills them in with a light brown. When she gets excited—which is usually when talking about boys—she talks quickly. "There was always lots of boys and beer and parties. [The gang] was all girls but we'd go and have parties in motels with boys from other gangs."

"We were always going out together—me and my other girls in the gang because we always had to go out with a lot of people in case something happened," Chapparo explains. What she means by this is that there was always the possibility they'd run into some *Nortenos*, in which case a fight would almost certainly break out, and they'd have to make sure they had enough gang members to take on the *Nortenos*.

One of the *Nortenos* Chapparo used to fight is named Goofy. When I ask her why her gang name is Goofy she says, "I don't know, I guess I'm kind of funny." After getting into repeated trouble with the law, Goofy is now trying to get out of her gang. Instead of wearing the standard gang uniform that's both loose and similar to male gang member's clothes—a Ben Davies top, ironed Dickies pants, and Nike Cortezes—these days she wears mostly green clothes made by Old Navy.

Like Chapparo, Goofy joined a gang when she was twelve. She joined the *Nortenos* because she started dating a guy who was a member. "If my dad had still lived with us I would never have messed with gangs or nothing. But my mom had no control. And it was pretty kick back at first. We'd get into trouble, go and drink, get coked up."

Not only do gang girls go to extremes to prove that they are as tough as guys—drink, take drugs, commit car-jackings—but they also have to earn their respect by not sleeping around. This can be difficult for the gang girl, who is often seeking love and affection from the male gang members. Many girls who are initiated into gangs have to "shoot the dice," which means that they have to roll a set of dice and have sex with as many males as the number that comes up on the dice. But because Goofy was the girlfriend of one of the gang's leaders, she didn't have to sleep around, and she was respected.

For Goofy's best friend, however, it was a different story. She got laughed out of a gang after sleeping around. Though one of the gang members she had sex with was Goofy's boyfriend, Goofy holds her friend at fault.

"As a girl especially, you gotta earn your respect," Goofy says with the authority of someone who could pen the gang-girl version of *The Rules*. "If some guy in the gang tries to get on you, you can't be like, yeah. You have to play at least a little hard to get. If they know you're a ho, they're going to try to stick it to you big. But if they know you're going out with one of their homeboys, they'll be like, 'Oh, you're cool.'" When Goofy imitates a homeboy voice it's not very flattering; she makes the guys in her gang sound dumb, thuggish. And yet, she completely defers to the patriarchy they establish in the gang, and she admits if it weren't for the guys and the fact that her boyfriend was in the gang, she would never have become a gang girl.

JUMPING IN

When I meet La Happy, a seventeen-year-old ex-Blood from Los Angeles, the first thing she says to me is, "No matter how long you live you will never go through what I have gone through."

"You're right," I say, realizing that what she wants from me is not sympathy but respect. Talking with gang girls, I've become accustomed to the braggadocio. In fact, I've often had to double-check accounts with parole officers and rival gang members to distinguish the bragging from the bare facts: More than any other group of women I've interviewed, gang girls are prone to exaggeration. This isn't because they're natural born liars, but because their identity is so wrapped up, so dependent on the stories they tell, that sometimes their confidence is derived as much from their narrative embellishments as their colors.

Although her gang name was La Happy because she was always exuberant and a party girl, these days it takes a lot to make her smile. "The whole reason I got into the gang and stuff was because, like, both my parents were into speed really bad so they weren't really there for me." (When la Happy says "parents" she's referring to her father and her stepmother; her real mother died from a drug overdose when La Happy was two years old.) At around the age of nine La Happy started hanging out with the other kids in the neighborhood, most of whom were in the gang Bentral Valley Bloods, or B.V.B. The area La Happy lived in was called Central Valley, but because it was a Blood gang and the Bloods and the Crips fight each other, her gang wasn't allowed to use any word that had C in it. This sort of arbitrary rule helps to differentiate the gangs and to create a sense of order that is missing in their members' lives.

La Happy is Caucasian and has copper-tinted hair that brings out metallic flecks in her green eyes that seem to get bright with anger when she talks about her childhood. "My parents would be so tweaked out and stuff that when it came to dinnertime nobody was cooking dinner. I mean, me and my brother [who is one year older] practically raised ourselves. We were doing our own thing, you know—we had to, otherwise we'd starve. My mom was always trying to stab my dad and kill him and he tried to kill her, too."

The more La Happy's parents fought, the more she hung out with the Bentral Valley Bloods, drinking, doing drugs, and "kickin' it." At the age of twelve she was initiated into the gang. La Happy says of her fellow gang members: "We were like a family because we were pretty much the only family most of us had. I mean, from my experience, people who get into gangs the most are the people whose parents are all drugged up, or maybe they don't have parents—they live with their grandparents. They're just yearning for the love and attention that they don't get, and they want to fit in."

For the first part of the initiation to B.V.B., La Happy was jumped in: She had to walk down a line with sixteen girls on either side and take their beatings. Afterward she wasn't in the best condition but she says she was "always so doped up and stuff that it was like nothing." La Happy also had to sleep with a male gang member. It was her first time having sex and she ended up going out with the boy, which helped her preserve her respect among the other gang members. Even though she was only twelve, nobody she knew was a virgin so losing her virginity to get into a gang "wasn't a big thing."

In B.V.B. there was more than one initiation. In order to earn seniority B.V.B. members had to work their way up through various stages. Soon after her first initiation into the gang, La Happy completed the second initiation, which in her case, involved robbing a house. (The second initiation always entailed a crime, the nature of which was determined by the gang.) She was staying at a friend's house and she and the friend and another girl climbed over the fence and broke into the house next door. Both of the other girls had burglarized houses before so they knew what to do and, at the time, La Happy thought it was fun. They stole credit cards (which they later used), phones, televisions, VCRs, and stereos. Her friend's mother suspected something so La Happy was kicked out of the house, but she was never caught by the authorities.

As a reward for robbing a house, the gang gave La Happy a red bandana, or what is more commonly known as "the red rag." (Bloods carry red rags, which distinguishes them from their enemies, the Crips, whose rags are blue. *Nortenos* also carry red, while *Surenos* wear blue, but this doesn't mean that Bloods and *Nortenos* or Crips and *Surenos* are in any way associated. There are two different wars going on.) Because she had also stolen a gun from the house, she was prepared for the third stage of initiation, a drive-by. "We had this place where everybody hung out at night," La

Happy explains. "There was a lot of Crips who went in there so you'd just drive by and pop off your gun. You don't have to hit anybody, you pop it off in the air and see if you get away with it and that's the initiation." The danger of this act was that if you did shoot a Crip, the gang would try to find out who did it (and with all the aforementioned braggadocio, this wouldn't be too difficult) and then come after you.

After this final initiation, La Happy had earned seniority and, with it, the privilege of initiating new members into the gang. When she beat up on the new members during initiation she says she was just getting out hatred that she felt toward her parents and that it was like a release for her. She enjoyed initiating new members because it meant people wanted to be part of their gang, and "every little person helped."

Whereas La Happy's initiation into a gang was also an initiation into a life of other crimes, Alicia wasn't officially jumped in until she had already been involved in a life of crime and drugs. In fact, Alicia started her own gang in the bathrooms of juvenile hall.

It was after she first ran away that she was initiated into what she calls "the system." That is, the system of jails and juvenile halls and ranches and group homes, which she is all too familiar with. "Now I'm part of the system," she says, "and the problem is all I do is go in and out of jail and in and out and in and out."

Alicia was fourteen when she got sent to juvenile hall for stealing a car. She says that she and her friends had stolen thirty cars before they got caught—mostly Buicks and Oldsmobiles because they're common and therefore their parts are easy to sell and hard to trace. Sometimes they'd steal two or three cars a day, she claims, and always during the day because that's when people least expect it. They make the mistake of thinking bad things only happen at night.

"It was me and my homeboy, Rest in Peace—he got killed. (He's now referred to as Rest in Peace by the gang.) They killed him at a party. It was him, his sister, and me, and some other friends. We used to steal cars—we used to go, like, to faraway places, steal cars, bring them back, and then strip 'em. And then take everything that we thought was good, you know—we'd take it and then sell it. That's how we got our alcohol, our weed, or all the things we wanted. And, I don't know, it used to be so fun and then the first time we ever stole a car from the closest place [we went]—we get caught. And, it's funny now, but it wasn't funny then, it was like we were at a movie or something like that because cops just came out of nowhere and we were just in the middle and there was just cops all around us. They came out of nowhere and it was like they had guns pointing at us and we had to have our hands up touching the ceiling of the car and stuff. And then, it was weird, we had to get on our knees, and we got off the car. I mean they really did us right there." Although Alicia describes the encounter with the police as being like something out of a movie, perhaps this is only because that's what she wishes it was. When talking about the arrest Alicia becomes uncharacteristically scared and sits up straight, as though she's witnessing a disturbing sight at too close a range, but can't turn away however much she may want to.

A girl in juvenile hall knew Alicia was hanging out with a gang called S.F.S., or San Francisco *Surenos,* and she wanted to get jumped in. Alicia didn't want to claim San Francisco since she wasn't from there. "I didn't feel right, you know. I'll claim south, but I won't claim San Francisco," explains Alicia. One of the girls who had started S.F.S. was in juvenile hall at the same time and Alicia talked to her and they decided to change the name to B.A.S., or Bay Area *Surenos.* "So we changed it to that, and then everybody agreed because everybody was from different areas—Daly City, San Francisco, Mountain View, East Palo Alto—and it just didn't make sense claiming San Francisco if you wasn't from there, so we changed it to B.A.S. and that's how it is now."

After she and the other girl, L., decided to changed the name, they jumped each other in the bathroom. First it was Alicia with several girls on her, all of them hitting her. "But," she says, "we were all fighting. They were hitting me, and I was hitting them, you know. We jumped, like, four people in that day. And then my friend, P., she was at the door just watching [to see] if the counselors would come. And then as soon as the counselors would come we would jump into the toilet [stalls] or [stand by] the sink or act like we were doing something in the bathroom, you know. The day before we jumped people in we'd have to play it off like we didn't get along with certain girls so in case someone did turn us in we'd be like, 'Well we don't even get along with them.' That way they wouldn't even know we'd gotten jumped in. 'Cause we could've gotten time for that."

Alicia and the newly formed B.A.S. continued initiating people both inside and outside the walls of juvenile hall. "[B.A.S.] was supposed to be just a female thing, you know, all female. But then we started having boyfriends and they kicked it with us and wanted to be in it—not in it—but they were down for us. So we were like 'fine, you know, let's all consider each other, you know, family.' So that's how B.A.S. really started. Now when we jump in a female, there's always one guy in there [helping to beat her up]. And there's always a girl, or two probably—because supposedly girls are weak— there's like one or two girls there to jump in a guy." Because B.A.S. was not originally a male gang, however, sex is not part of the initiation ritual.

Alicia says she felt terrible the first time she jumped someone into B.A.S.: "I felt so bad because we messed up that little girl. I mean she's not little—she's seventeen—but she is so small. She is four something and she is so skinny she's like a little stick, you know. It was four of us on her, you know, and after us four, it was another three, you know. We jumped her in, right, but we didn't jump her in in front of everybody, so then another three people had to jump her in in front of everybody."

Unlike La Happy's gang, B.A.S. doesn't require that the girls sleep with the boys to get into the gang, nor does it have official stages one has to go through to earn seniority. However, gang members still have to show that they are down for each other, that they'll do anything that another gang member asks of them. Alicia's friend, L., with whom Alicia founded B.A.S., is in prison until 2001 because she wanted to show how down she was for the gang. L. was charged with kidnapping an old woman and keeping her hostage in a trunk and doing an armed robbery on a liquor store. L. was in the liquor store with another girl from the gang and the girl told her, "If you're down for the gang, you'll do a 2-11." (A 2-11 is the police code for armed robbery. Gang members are often so familiar with the repercussions of their crimes that they'll refer to them by their police codes. What this suggests is that more important than the crime itself is the penalty the members will risk—all in the name of showing their loyalty to the gang.) Without hesitating, L. stabbed the woman who was working the cash register in her side, stole the money in the register, and ran out. Alicia says L. will probably end up getting more years added to her sentence because she recently beat up another girl in prison so badly that the girl almost died. As a result, L. is now in solitary lock-down.

Despite L.'s actions, or rather, because of them, Alicia sees L. as really being there for the gang. "I don't think of her as a bad person, I see her like she was really down, you know," Alicia says. "She was down for the hood, down for us, that's how I see it. She was one out of a thousand people who would do something for a person, someone who didn't think before reacting, just did it. If you tell her, 'Steal your mom's car,' she would probably do it. She would do anything for her homies and for the hood, you know. If we needed something and nobody could get it, she'd find a way, just for her to be down." Now, L.'s homegirls send drugs to her in prison because, as Alicia explains, "She was down for them, so they're down for her."

. . .

While there's no official rush period to join a gang, and no national Pan-Hellenic office to assure that certain procedures are followed, gang initiations all over the country are strikingly similar. This has to do with the fact that a lot of gang knowledge is exchanged in prison (a lot of gang girls I talked to, joined or formed their own gangs while locked up) and because, according to Jose Rosado, an ex-gang member himself who is now in the Bronx, New York, helping kids get out of gangs through a project called Youth Force, a lot of New York City gang members get their knowledge of gangs from movies like *Menace to Society* and *Dead Homies*.

While the gangs in New York are different from those in California—there's the Latin Kings and Queens, and the Netas—recently there's been a growing phenomenon in New York City of young people taking on the symbols, colors, and initiation rites of the Bloods, and the police know of at least six hundred people organized into at least sixteen subsets of the gang. In New York, many gang initiations take on California themes, but with a twist. For example, instead of drive-by shootings, many East Coast Blood initiates engage in subway slayings. (I know of a woman with red hair who was held at knifepoint by five girl-gang members on the train to Brooklyn one night because, as they said, she was wearing their color.) Unlike the California Bloods, however, New York City gang members in one part of the city are just as likely to fight Bloods from another part as they are likely to fight Crips.

"This is not a case where the Crip or Blood travel agency sent these guys down here and told them to start a gang," Jeffrey Fagan, a gang expert and the director of Columbia University's Center for Violence Research and Prevention told the *New York Times*. "These guys are imitating gang culture because it provides instant status and reputation in communities where reputation and status have very exaggerated—and often life or death—meaning."

The girls in New York are more violent than the males, Rosado explains, because the gang girls get into vicious fights with each other over their boyfriends. If having respect in a gang means having a gangster boyfriend, then these girls are going to fight for their men. The desire for respect also often influences their decision of what initiation trial to go through: They're often given a choice of playing shoot the dice or committing a crime, and most opt for the latter. (Rosado tells me of going to prison to visit the girl who was responsible for the well-publicized 1997 murder of a New York City taxi driver. She did it, many believe, to get into a Blood gang.)

Rosado, who's lived on both coasts and has a tattoo of tears near his left eye, the symbol the Netas use to represent their grief over their members who are in prison (Netas started as a pro-inmates rights movement), says that East Coast gangs are different from California gangs in other ways aside from the initiations. "East Coast gangs are more wanna-be. People join them for the money or because they're wanna-be gangsters. In New York, you join a gang by choice—you're either in or you're out. In California, belonging to a gang is a religion, it's a way of life."

GETTING OUT

La Happy has a story she likes to tell to show how being in a gang puts everybody in danger. "A long time ago when I first got that gun [from the robbery] my little brother, Johnny, and I shared a room and I had the gun under my mattress. And I was teaching him crap, like we used to have this saying, 'Chitty chitty, bang bang, it's all about the Blood gang,' and I was teaching it and things like that, and he ended up getting a hold of my gun because he had seen everything that I'd done. He ended up chasing my friend Eric down the street with the gun. It was loaded. He could have got hurt. My brother was three years old." Although I don't know any three-year-old who can chase people down the street, I see what La Happy's getting at. Not only was Eric at risk because of La Happy's gun, but her brother was also growing up fast.

La Happy also has a story about Eric and the dangers of being in a gang, but it's a story she doesn't like to tell. "Eric was one of the heads of the gang. We were sitting out in front of his house one night and we had just done a couple of lines of speed. We were tweaking. And these two people that we knew who lived right around the corner that Eric had grown up with, right—they got really drunk, and really smashed and they came over. Eric and one of the guys started arguing. I was sitting on the back of the car and Eric was sitting on my lap.

"One of the guys that was there,—he was in B.V.B., too—wanted total authority over the gang, and to get total authority you have to knock out the person that was the authority, which was Eric. Eric was only thirteen, but his dad was the leader before his dad passed away. So then it was left to Eric. So J. and C. came up and they just started arguing with Eric. And it looked like they were hittin' Eric. I couldn't really see because it was dark, but one of the people was hittin' him, and [it turns out] they were stabbing him.

"[Eric] was right in front of me and he just got up. He started walking towards the house and I looked and just saw his shirt turning completely red and I was just like, 'Oh my God,' and then he started falling to the ground and he grabbed my hand and goes, 'What, you don't love me any more?' right before he fell. And then I ran into the house and told them to call somebody because Eric got stabbed." La Happy pauses for a long while. She twists her watch around her wrist nervously. "Eric got flied to the hospital and he's a complete vegetable now. They stabbed him in the heart and in the lungs. He's completely paralyzed; he can't talk."

The behavior La Happy started witnessing in her gang is the same behavior that she witnessed in her own family. She grew up watching her parents try to stab each other and she sought refuge in a gang, only to find her fellow gang members stabbing each other. La Happy says that Eric's question "What, you don't love me any more?" was addressed to her. But his question is one that many gang members address to their families before they join gangs, and one that, more and more, they find themselves asking their fellow gang members as the gang starts to disintegrate.

B.V.B. started to fall apart after Eric was stabbed. "Everybody was going against each other," La Happy says. "I mean, B.V.B. was going against B.V.B. and it was just a bunch of crap." The boy La Happy had to have sex with as part of her initiation into B.V.B. got himself killed by trying to leave the gang. "I think it was getting too much for him," La Happy explains. "I mean B.V.B.—we were falling apart and he went over to C.V.C. because they were the ones making us fall apart and he got shot. You can't just walk out of a gang."

"There is no more B.V.B. anymore. It just wore itself out. Everybody's either in prison, or they're dead. It was pretty much easy for me to get out of the gang because it disintegrated on its own, but a lot of other people don't really have a choice. I mean, you can get out of a gang, but you gotta move. You gotta move with no trace, you know. A lot of people who are in gangs, their families don't have enough money to do something like that. Most of the families are on welfare or whatever."

As for La Happy, she's almost off probation. The only visible signs that she was once in a gang are her tattoo of the initials of the boy who was killed when he tried to leave B.V.B., the same boy who helped initiate her into the gang, and the "B.V.B." that is carved into her wrist. She now wears a watch around her wrist to cover it up. When La Happy is nervous, which is usually when she's talking about her future, she twists the watch around her wrist in circles, as though it, or what it's concealing, is still a shackle of sorts.

La Happy plans to marry another ex-gang member, as soon as she turns eighteen. For the ceremony they want to go to a casino resort in Reno called the Silver Legacy because they like the television commercial for it. In the commercial, the voice of what is supposed to be the ghost of a gold miner says something along the lines of "I've always had a dream to build this palace, and now that dream has come true." Perhaps the commercial appeals to La Happy because she hopes that she and her fiancé can build a new life together. They plan to move to a small town where there aren't any gangs.

We're sitting at a picnic table in a quiet, nongang territory in Los Angeles and she places her hands on the table that's carved, not with gang names but with "I wuz here"s and various proclamations of love. La Happy says one piece of advice she would give a gang girl is that there are three streets you can go down when you're in a gang. "You go down this street, you're going to die," she says. With her finger she draws a line on the table that veers toward her left. "You go down this one, you're going to be in prison." Again she draws a path, this time heading straight in front of her. "But, you go down this one, you're going to be free," she says as she lifts her hand up off the table and out to her right. She stares in the direction of her finger for a moment. La Happy isn't pointing to any place in particular when she says the word "free," just somewhere very far away.

"Our gang is so different from other gangs," Alicia says. "We treat others with respect. As soon as you treat us with disrespect, we disrespect." This motto of Alicia's gang, not coincidentally, also sums up her relationship with her own family. The reason she says she started getting involved with gangs in the first place is because she was having problems with her family telling her what to do and not trusting her after they found her with drugs. So when she thought they were showing her disrespect, she ran away.

Part of the attraction of a gang to Alicia is that the members are always down for her if she's down for them. She says that she warns potential gang members that if they want to join, they better be down for the gang. Or else. She tells one story about a girl, M., who was jumped into B.A.S. in juvenile hall, and then once she was out of juvenile hall, claimed the enemy gang of *Nortenos*. So Alicia and her friend "got her." Alicia says, "We just messed her up. And from there on, she was like, 'I don't gang bang. I don't gang bang.' So she thinks she's jumped out, but she's not jumped out. (Curiously, gang members use the same procedure, i.e., beating someone up, when kicking a member out of the gang—"jumping them out"—as they do when initiating them, or "jumping them in.") We're waiting for my homegirl to get out of prison because she's the one we jumped M. in with. Then we're going to jump M." Alicia says that she warns people before they join B.A.S that if they're going to be another M., that is, if they're going to switch gangs, they should leave there and then, before they get themselves in a lot of trouble.

Despite her desire for the gang to be down for one another, Alicia says that gang life has changed: "These days everything's different. Your own friends are like your enemies and stuff. If they see something that you've got and they ain't got, even though they're your friends, they'll take it from you or they'll just get other people to do it for them so it won't make it seem like it's them, but it's them, you know. In a way it's sad, because everyone that used to hang around is mostly enemies now. You talk to this person and they'll be like, 'Oh, you talk to her still?' and I'm all, 'Yeah,' and they'll be, like, 'Why do you talk to her? She's all this and this and this.' "

"These days, everybody does what they want to show everybody that they're better than anybody else. They'll do anything to prove that they're everything." Alicia believes that things were different in the days of the O.G.s, or Old Gangsters. "[Then] it was like 'hands up,' you know—just fight, not kill, just less violent. Yeah, they killed and stuff but not as much as they do these days. These days you look at somebody wrong and they're like, 'I'm going to shoot you.' It's like that gun's already in your face."

CHAPTER FIVE

Spellbound: Witches

It's Halloween night, 1997, and I'm in Salem, Massachusetts, with a bunch of witches. Not the typical coven of "sexy witches" often spotted at October 31 costume parties (you know the type, girls who opt to wear little black dresses instead of pumpkin outfits), but women *and* men, who believe they are actual witches—and not just on Halloween. I'm talking about people who celebrate Samhain, the witches' New Year, when the souls of the dead are believed to revisit their loved ones. I'm talking about people who are into Wicca.

Wicca is a federally recognized religion whose devotees usually describe their faith as a revival of primitive pagan rituals that predate Judeo-Christian tradition—rituals that celebrated the earth, sun, moon, and goddesses rather than a god. Some observers of these ancient holidays call themselves pagans, others call themselves witches, and the way it works is that all witches are pagans, but not all pagans are witches. Get it? The reason all these witches, pagans, and I are outside of a Salem store called the Raven's Nest, which sells pagan books and supplies (incense, herbs, swords, etc.) is that we're waiting for the Samhain ritual to begin.

About fifty people have shown up for what the Raven's Nest calls its neowitchcraft circle.[1] Most of the participants are women, many of them are young. Unlike everyone else in Salem who's dressed in a costume, the only outfits these people are wearing are dark frocks of one sort or another and almost all of them have tattoos or pendants depicting pentacles. Pentacles are the star-like five-pointed symbol of paganism. The five points represent the five elements: fire, air, water, earth, and essence. I try talking to a girl with dyed black hair and a cape, a student at the college in Salem—I get as far as that—but when I persist in asking her about her beliefs she looks at me as though conjuring up a spell, and so I retreat. I have better luck with the next three girls I approach. Unlike the three witches in *Macbeth*, these three witches don't talk about killing swine, or say things like "Fair is foul, and foul is fair" or "By the pricking of my thumbs, something wicked this way comes." In fact, after conversing with the three witches for a while and hearing their stories, I note that behind their whitened faces and black kohl-rimmed eyes, they are fragile, innocent girls—which is perhaps precisely why many of them have become witches.

FIRST WITCH

Liz, who's eighteen, has dark black hair that hangs around her head in letter Js. She's wearing a black dress and black knee-high boots. A waitress in New Jersey, Liz first got into Wicca at the age of twelve, when her brother introduced her to it.

---

[1]Generally, pagan rituals begin with what is known as the "casting of a circle," which circumscribes a sacred space. According to Starhawk, author of *The Spiral Dance*, a book of witchcraft rituals and invocations, the casting of a circle "establishes a temple in the heart of the forest or the center of a convener's living room. Goddess and God are then invoked or awakened within each participant and are considered to be physically present within the circle and the bodies of the worshippers. Power, the subtle force that shapes reality is raised through chanting or dancing and may be directed through a symbol or visualization. With the raising of the cone of power comes ecstasy, which may then lead to a trance state in which visions are seen and insights gained. Food and drink are shared, and coveners 'earth the power' and relax, enjoying a time of socializing. At the end, the powers invoked are dismissed, the circle is opened, and a formal return to ordinary consciousness is made."

"I started reading a lot of Books of Shadows [journals that other witches have kept] and when I felt ready, I initiated myself. I picked a deity I felt comfortable with, which in my case was Diana, because her symbol is the moon and she's a strong female deity. I drew a circle, said a prayer, made an oath not to harm anyone and to learn from enlightenment. I said it aloud and then drew blood from my finger in front of an altar."

Since then Liz has performed rituals every full moon and every time she's "had a bad day." When I ask her how being a witch has been different from what she expected, she looks disappointed and tells me, "It's not as dramatic as I thought it would be. I thought people would react to it differently—more dramatically."

"But sometimes being a witch is dangerous," she says, and her eyes light up. "Sometimes when I'm outside doing my rituals—I like being outside because you have the earth and everything living around you and it's easier to feel it—I light a fire in my circle and the police come and I run away!"

SECOND WITCH

Alexis is a lithe, blond twenty-year-old with a nose ring in her left nostril and big brown eyes that make me think of Clara from *The Nutcracker*. She looks at everything around her with wonder. She first got interested in Wicca when she was sixteen, when a friend gave her a book about it. "I started going to more stores where I met people, but I still didn't really believe it until I did a spell. I sat in my room and did a special vigil calling out to a distant friend to contact me. That week, a friend I hadn't talked to in a long time called me.

"It made me feel that somebody was out there listening to me, that there was someone who was there for me." Of course, the somebody out there who she felt was listening to her wasn't the friend who called, but the religion of Wicca itself. "I never believed anybody was out there listening, because I had never gotten *results*. But then, maybe I was in the wrong religion before, because this one worked for me." Her use of the word *results* makes me think of commercials with spokeswomen talking about a product that will help you shed those pounds, at last, or finally get your dining room table to gleam.

Alexis practiced on her own for a while and last year she started going to group ritual ceremonies. "But I still do a lot of personal rituals. Usually spells for home security, or money. Right now I've been doing spells to try to find an apartment."[2]

Her pager goes off and she looks at the number, "It's a 911 from my boyfriend. He's a witch too. He probably wants to wish me a good Samhain," she explains to me, clips her pager on the waistband of her long, silky black skirt, and turns back to our conversation. I wonder to myself if she and her boyfriend resorted to this technological device (the pager) to expedite communication; after all, when Alexis used a spell to get in touch with a friend it took almost a week for the friend to get back to her.

"As long as I have some type of spirituality, that's what's important in life. It's important to know something's working for me."[3]

THIRD WITCH

Aside from the pentacle that hangs from a cord around her neck, Lindsey looks like a young Marilyn Monroe wanna-be. A twenty-three-year-old florist in Manhattan, she first got interested in what she calls "spirituality" when she was thirteen. "I was in a foster home

---

[2]These spells have been more ambiguously effective. When I call Alexis at the boarding house she's been staying at, her landlady informs me that Alexis and her boyfriend, several months behind in rent, recently skipped out in the middle of the night.

[3]After the incident with the landlady, I try contacting Alexis via her beeper, but am informed that it's no longer in service. It's not that I feel a need to keep in touch with Alexis, but rather the opposite. Of all the girls I've interviewed for this book, it is the witches who are most needy, most innocent, and the most dependent on keeping up some sort of relationship with me. Once, when Alexis was still living at the boarding house, I was remiss in calling her and when I called a week late, I was chastised by her boyfriend who said, "She was really upset when you didn't call. On the verge of tears."

for two years in high school and I would spend a lot of time alone. So I would play with things like crystals and Ouija boards. I became addicted to Ouija boards, which is harmful because you kind of make things up."

At eighteen Lindsey was introduced to Wicca by a girl she met at a party. "I was at a point in my life where I kept getting hurt. Like I would take in bad roommates, people who were going through a rough time, and they would just shit on me. But being involved in Wicca has taught me how to turn the negative into a positive. Because it all comes back to, like, your karma."

Lindsey likes being part of spiral dances, like the one they'll do tonight in Salem, because they make her "feel one with other people" but she believes all religions are fundamentally private and that Wicca is all about being one with yourself. On her own, Lindsey performs full moon, personal, and meditative rituals. "Basically, I do rituals almost twenty times a month," she explains. "I often say prayers for people. I think good thoughts and hope that with my love and caring, people will make it through things. People need that energy. It's like when you like a boy and you find out that he's been thinking about you for no reason, and it feels really good. I try to think about everybody who's been good to me."

"Wicca is like a little angel that hovers over you," she says. "The elements—earth, fire, water, and air—they're always there for you." When no one else is, I think.

Listening to these witches' stories about the rituals they perform, I picture girls blowing on dandelions and wishing for something; I think of high school girls turning over "wish cigarettes"—that one cigarette they'll smoke last in the pack they hide from their parents—believing that when they smoke it their dreams will come true. In many ways, Wicca is no different from dandelion dreams or wish cigarettes—after all, "guidebooks" to Wicca like Starhawk's *Spiral Dance* include rituals for protection, loneliness, and being one with your womb, as well as herbal charm recipes to attract money or love, to heal a broken heart, for protection, to get a job, for inner power, for eloquence, and to win in court. But young women take Wicca more seriously than wishing on shooting stars because to them it is a religion, it is a coherent philosophy. As if by magic, simply by becoming witches, they feel that there is something out there looking after them.

In other words, as Second Witch Alexis says, by practicing Wicca, they get results. This emphasis on getting results seems quite commercial for a religion that's supposed to take you back to nature. But much of Wicca is fundamentally consumer-based. Instead of churches, occult stores provide most of the "counseling" and information that would-be witches seek. They also sell all the supplies: herbs, candles, cauldrons, crystals, swords, athames (knives used to cut things in the astral plane—where the souls of the dead reside; thus, the athame is an important tool on Samhain—and to cut cloth, cords, or candles used in rituals), stones, and spell books.

Even the process of choosing Wicca as a religion is often similar to the process of shopping. "People who are looking for alternative religions often turn to Wicca because it's easy to integrate into your life," says Chris, owner of the Raven's Nest, the occult store in Salem, and high priest of the Samhain Circle. "Wicca isn't as inaccessible as some of the more exotic religions, like Hinduism for example."

When I ask if the Raven's Nest advertises, Heather, the high priestess of the circle and Chris's girlfriend, tells me that they don't. "People just seem to come to Salem from all over the world and find us," Heather explains. "It's very magical."

Gerald Gardner founded Wicca in England in the 1940s. He based the religion's name on the Celtic word for the elders in primitive societies who used herbs and magical spells to heal and cure, and argued that Wicca was an ancient religion, passed down unchanged from pagan times. But scholars may tell you otherwise. "There are some practitioners who say that what we call paganism today is a continuous practice, but we have no evidence that that is true," said Wendy Griffin, an associate professor of women's studies at California State University at Long Beach in a 1996 interview with the *Los Angeles Times*. Many practitioners call it neopaganism in recognition of this fact. While paganism may be thousands of years old, Griffin and other academics argue, Wicca is very young.

So are an increasing number of its practitioners, who range from high school students seeking direction from more than just their Ouija boards to women's studies majors at Smith. Because no established temples exist (except for Mother Earth herself) there's no accurate count of how many young women practice Wicca. And while some estimate that there are half a million practicing pagans in the country today (the *New York Times* says the number of American Wiccans is between 50,000 and 300,000), J. Gordon Melton, director of the Institute of American Religions, estimates that the number is probably closer to 60,000 to 70,000. After all, there are those who are no longer practicing.

Melton, who has been studying Wiccan and neopagan groups for over twenty-five years, says that when Wicca started to spread from England to America in the 1960s, males held the majority of prominent leadership positions. Since then, however, he's witnessed the exclusively female sector of Wicca growing—many feminists embrace witchcraft because they believe male authority is still trying to suppress strong women, just as it did in the sixteenth and seventeenth centuries. Melton agrees with me that this increase in the feminist sector of Wicca—as evidenced by newsletters and visible groups—along with the Internet, movies like *The Craft* and TV shows like *Sabrina, the Teenage Witch* and *Charmed*, has attracted younger women to Wicca today.

Even publishers noticed a surge in sales of witch books among teens after the release of *The Craft*. Llewellyn Publications, a publishing house based in St. Paul, published a book entitled *Teen Witch* to capitalize on the new readership created by the film. "Our typical reader had been a boomer who grew up in the sixties who had been looking for a more appealing explanation of spirituality," Von Brashler, Llewellyn's director of trade sales, told the *New York Times* in a 1998 interview. "Now our typical reader is becoming a very young woman in her teens."

Look at any high school and you will see witches haunting the hallways. Teachers in places as diverse as San Antonio, Texas, Marin County, California, and New York City have told me about the sudden appearance—as if by magic—of witches in their classrooms. In its 1997 "Girl Issue," *Spin* magazine published a compendium of fifty-six archetypes of women, ranging from Christina Ricci to Freida Kahlo to Lisa Simpson, who have "helped define Girl Culture." Witches ranked number one. *Spin* explained Wicca's popularity thusly: "Aside from all the incense burning and cat fetishization, much of Wicca's appeal lies in its incredibly feminist doctrine: Wiccans believe a goddess created the universe and that women can control their own destinies." The feminist doctrine that these younger witches espouse is less that of the older witches', and more of the "Girls Kick Ass" and "Chicks Rule" variety. Think of these young witches' beliefs as second-wave Wicca.

Of course, witchcraft is nothing new. In sixteenth-and seventeenth-century Europe, between 40,000 and nine million women (depending on which historian's account you read) were accused of witchcraft and many were burned alive. Reasons women were suspected of witchcraft ranged from social slights (the townsperson who wasn't invited to a wedding or christening and showed resentment was often held responsible for subsequent marriage or childrearing problems) to economic competition (if times are hard, and you believe in spells, it's not unthinkable that the unpleasant neighbor is responsible for whatever goes wrong).

What's curious about the emergence of Wicca is that historically the identity of a witch was not one that was chosen, but rather imposed by suspicious villagers. It was an identity that many died refusing to take on. However, as Alison Lurie wrote in an article on witchcraft that appeared in *The New York Review of Books*, while many accused witches denied the charge, or confessed only under torture, some accepted the role of witch without even having been accused. "After all," Lurie rationalizes, "if you already believe in witches, and the curses you utter in a moment of rage or resentment come true, maybe you're one of them. And if you have good reason to be angry, envious, or resentful—if you're poorer and less lucky than your neighbors—the idea that you have special powers can be attractive."

Similarly, young women initiated into Wicca today aren't "accused" of being witches, but rather take on the role voluntarily. Becoming a witch is relatively easy. There are no tests to pass, no curtsey to perfect, no rush week, no getting beat up. Also, once you become a witch, there aren't a lot of rules. "What I like about Wicca is that there's no set dogma," says one young witch named Willow who learned about Wicca on the Internet. As with more traditional religions, you can be initiated into Wicca at any age. And its doctrinal flexibility results in both diverse practitioners and a diversity of practices. Some witches are "solitaries" who practice alone; others join a coven.[4] Some join covens that have males and females ("Wicca is a religion, not an all-girl's club," another young witch tells me), others only want to practice with other women. A few regard the Wicked Witch of the West as their role model; others abhor her.

According to Melton, part of the reason the word *witchcraft* was originally chosen by the priests and prophets of this new religion

---

[4]This from Starhawk's *Spiral Dance*: "The coven is a Witch's support group, consciousness-raising group, psychic study center, clergy-training program, College of Mysteries, surrogate clan, and religious congregation all rolled into one. In a strong coven, the bond is, by tradition, 'closer than family': a sharing of spirits, emotions, imaginations. 'Perfect love and perfect trust' are the goal." According to her, "Covens are autonomous, free to use whatever rituals, chants, and invocations they prefer. There is no set prayer book of liturgy."

was because it was a loaded word. "It attracted attention," Melton told the *L.A. Times*. "You might not be interested in 'an Earth-based religion,' but 'witchcraft' carried an immediate connotation." Young women often take on the identity of witch for much the same reason—it sets them apart from the others in their school and instills in them the sort of beefed-up confidence and the ability to shock that helps them navigate their way through the rough seas of young adulthood.

Wiccans and other pagans follow an agriculturally based calendar. Most perform thirteen Esbats (full-moon ceremonies) and eight Sabbats (solar festivals that celebrate the changing of the seasons). Samhain (Halloween, October 31) is just one of these Sabbats on which Wiccans and pagans perform communal rituals—the other seven are Yule (Winter Solstice, December 21–23), Brigid (Candlemas, February 2), Eostar (Spring Equinox, March 20–23), Beltane (May Eve), Litha (Summer Solstice, June 20–23), Lughnasad (August 1), and Mabon (Fall Equinox, September 20–23)—but Samhain is the one Sabbat that almost every other American joins Wiccans in celebrating as well.

Each Halloween 200,000 people travel to Salem to visit the witch memorial and the wax museum and (primarily) drink in this town of 38,000 where the infamous witch trials took place in 1692. A handful of these visitors are girls who practice Wicca and for whom Salem is Mecca. "Being here in Salem I feel in touch with my roots," one girl dressed in, of course, black tells me. Does she come from a family tradition of being put on trial and being burned at the stake? I wonder. More likely, she's referring to the roots of who she wants to be. "It's like how Italians living in America must feel when they go back to Rome."

The first three women accused of being witches in seventeenth-century Salem were Tituba, a Caribbean Indian slave, servant to the Reverend Parris, who accused her of practicing palmistry and teaching it to the reverend's daughter and her friends; Sarah Good, a disreputable woman who wandered through the Salem Streets smoking a pipe and begging for money; and Sarah Osborne, who had failed to attend church regularly and was suspected of immoral acts. During the course of the Salem witch trials fifty-five people, with the help of torture, eventually confessed to being witches. The number who show up for the open Samhain circle at the Raven's Nest comes close to that, but they've come of their own accord.

At nine o'clock the circle is drawn, which means that high priest Chris takes an athame (the knife) and literally draws a circle around the altar. Chris is wearing a black cloak, and high priestess Heather is dressed in a burgundy velvet gown. Chris talks about how Samhain is the passing from one world to the next and asks the group that is gathered to concentrate on people who have died and what they would say to them if they were here today. Then he creates a circle of light (this time by looking up at the dark sky and drawing a circle with the athame). There's drumming and incense—this is when you're supposed to be communicating with the dead—and everyone begins to chant, "The circle is open, never to be unbroken/ May the light of the goddess / Be ever in our hearts."

The circle is on a grassy knoll, next to a crowded bar, and as the drumming gets more intense and the ritual reaches its pinnacle in pitch and fervor, some uninvited guests stumble up to the circle's perimeter. These include a man dressed as Homer Simpson, a man sporting a large Budweiser beer can costume, and a woman dressed like Hester Prynne with a big 'A' on her dress.

"Wow, it smells like crap," says Homer Simpson sniffing the incense.

"What is this, a powwow?" says the Budweiser can.

Hester Prynne announces, "This is depressing."

Liz, the girl who relishes running away from the police, turns to the threesome, puts her arms at her side, palms facing down, fingers outward, and glares. This heavy stare, I realize, is intended to symbolize to all onlookers that Liz is activating her magic powers to repel the uninvited guests, and I think of the personalized "magic-activation" gestures cultivated by others who have taken on the role of witch before her, e.g., Samantha Stephens's (*Betwitched*) nose-wiggle and Sabrina's (*Sabrina, The Teenage Witch*) finger-pointing. This is what Liz has been waiting for: the opportunity to make others feel like outsiders. Call it a witch's revenge.

For Halloween, fifteen-year-old Julie dressed up as a Catholic school girl because "Catholic school girls always dress up like witches." Julie, you see, is a witch. Not having been initiated yet, she's not a full-fledged witch but she's looking forward to her initiation, to what she calls "coming out of the broom closet" so that the identity she's found so rewarding to assume can be made permanent, so that her parents will stop thinking it's just a phase she's going through. Not unlike her hippie, rocker, and Buddhist phases, I imagine.

I meet Julie through Enchantments, an occult store in New York's East Village that offers classes, or what are called "groves" to people who want to learn more about Wicca and paganism. For legal reasons, stores like Enchantments are cautious of initiating any minors, and so Julie won't be initiated by Joe, the high priest at the store, until she is eighteen. Actually, until she is eighteen and one day— the one day comes from the Wiccan belief that you must study for at least a year and a day before you can be initiated.

I have signed up for the grove to get a sense of what sort of person joins these things, and I find a definite divide among the class of some forty-odd people. The over-thirty crowd generally turns to Wicca because, as they explain it, they feel they were "born witches" or because they've "been on this road their entire life but just didn't know what it was called." The younger, sub-twenty-one-year-old girls say they want to be witches because they "want to shock their friends and get back at people." One even says she wants to be a witch "to seek empowerment over my eating disorder."

I offer to take Julie for coffee one day and leave the choice of a locale up to her. To my (initial) surprise, despite our proximity to a number of gothic-decored coffee shops, Julie selects Starbucks. She's wearing all black and her hair is dyed black, and her lipstick looks as though she's had a lot of red wine to drink, except that later she tells me when she performs rituals she doesn't drink wine. Instead, she drinks apple juice out of her ritual goblet. Among the yuppies at Starbucks, Julie stands out—and this, I realize as we continue to talk, is the point.

"I lived in the suburbs until I was fourteen," she tells me, and spoons some whipped cream from the top of her hot chocolate into her mouth. "I told myself, 'When I move to the city, I'm going to change. I'm going to be more outgoing, I'm going to be myself.' I didn't want to be part of the status quo any longer. I didn't want to be a boring, blank person."

And how have things changed now that she's no longer bland in appearance?

"Sometimes on the subway old women will move away from me. Sometimes when I'm walking down the street people will spit at my feet. But I find it amusing. I get kicks out of it. I'm showing my originality and who I am. I like challenging people's perceptions."

On her backpack, in which she lugs around her sophomore textbooks—most of them science books—are seven pins. Five of the pins have witch slogans: "Where there's a witch there's a way"; "Born again pagan"; "Life's a witch when you fly"; "My Goddess gave birth to your goddess"; and "Eve was framed." The other two pins are of a witch's head, the evil kind of witch from *The Wizard of Oz*, and a pentacle, the five-point star. She wears five necklaces around her neck, all hanging from black cords of varying lengths, so that the pendants sit one on top of the other, like heads on a totem pole. The five necklaces are a Celtic knot, a tree of life (representing eternity), a pentacle, a goddess (which she says represents gay rights), and a quartz cat.

Julie first became intrigued by Wicca through her interest in the European and Salem Inquisitions. When I ask her what she likes most about Wicca she says, "It's given me a community." This community is very much a family to her, and she calls members of it her "Craft sister" or her "Craft daddy." "Most important of all," Julie continues, "Wicca has given me *something* to believe in."

Julie and others employ the derogatory term "Crafties" to refer to poser witches, i.e., those who have seen the movie *The Craft* about four girls who become friends and become powerful because of their experimentation with witchcraft, and think they can do the same. The desire to show that one is not a Craftie, that one is a serious, real witch, often leads young women to extreme Wicca initiations.

In the witch trials of 1692 Tituba confessed that when she signed Satan's book she saw nine other names in the book, but she could only remember two. And so began the frenzy of finding Tituba's co-signers. Although young witches today don't sign Satan's book, within covens they have to go through some sort of initiation to become a witch. Usually this initiation merits its own ritual and being branded with the coven's secret symbol. Although there are no prescribed initiations, many use Starhawk's initiation ritual as a blueprint for their own. As she describes in *The Spiral Dance*, most initiations involve a test (finding one's way along an unknown path), a ritual bath (if the initiation is outside, a running stream or ocean is ideal; if held indoors, a bathtub will do), a series of challenging questions such as "Are you willing to suffer to learn?", the subsequent pricking of the initiate's finger to draw blood, and swearing on one's mother's womb to never reveal the secrets of the coven.

Relations among coven members are not always harmonious, and covens seem to have a break-up rate greater than that of rock bands. Oftentimes this is because one person assumes the position of leader—or high priest—in the group, and sooner or later the others want to overthrow him or her.

One leader of such a coven is Peter, who when not acting as high priest is a tarot-card reader in a mall in upstate New York. I meet him two days after Halloween at the fifteenth Annual NYC Halloween Witches Masquerade Ball at the Wetlands, a New York City club where I've seen bands play in the past. Tonight is different however, not only because there's a DJ, but because at midnight they'll do a circle dance.

The crowd at Wetlands is made up of old and young, dressed up and weirdly dressed. I'm there with a friend and she points out to me that the majority of guys at Wetlands, who are standing against the wall, their eyes looking magnified behind the thick lenses of their heavy glasses, are recognizable as the type of guy who was into Dungeons and Dragons when we were in high school in the eighties. Now, in the nineties, they're into the occult.

If the Wiccan guys are the former Dungeons and Dragons devotees, then who were the Wiccan girls in the 1980s? No predecessor comes to mind. My friend, who grew up in Seattle, is at a loss as well. And then it hits me: They were just normal girls. Maybe loners, maybe not. Girls who, as they got more lost, wanted something to believe in.

Dressed in black jeans and black boots and a collared black shirt, Peter looks more like a guy dressed to go out for a night in the city than a witch. Unlike the other men at Wetlands he looks like the cool guy in high school, and this might account for why he is the head of a coven with a substantial and devoted number of female members. Peter says he inherited the power to see within people from his ancestors, who were blacksmiths involved in Black Art in the Middle Ages. For example, he says of people who want to join his coven, "I observe them and I know when they're ready." His eyebrows arch and he looks like the evil figure in a cartoon, but he's not trying to be funny.

"When they're ready, the other members and I take them into the woods and we ingest a hallucinogenic—just like Native Americans would take peyote—and then we do some fire jumping and fertility rituals." While the fire jumping is a test of skill and devotion, the fertility rituals are purely a test of devotion. A female initiate must sleep with all the men and women in the coven. Then, and only then, are they let in on the coven's secrets and branded with a steel rod. The design of the brand is a secret, but Peter does tell me it is 2 inches by 1 inch and placed on the same spot on every member's body—his or her butt.

"All I know is that there's a change in a person once they've been initiated," Peter says. "Once your eyes are opened they're never closed again," he tells me in language similar to that of people describing a memorable drug trip, minus the added rituals. "Your eyes are opened forcibly from that point on."

While most covens do have rigorous initiation rituals and most involve branding, not all leaders of covens are as Mephistophelean as Peter. In fact, contrary to what I expected when I first started hanging out with witches—before I learned that many witches respect the words of Scott Cunningham, an author who wrote extensively about Wicca until he died in 1993, who said that because of Karma, whatever wish you send out comes back to you threefold—many covens refrain from performing evil. Most covens are less like Peter's and more like Karin's.

Karin is a costume designer who I meet at the same witches' ball where I meet Peter. She's come as an alien—one of her own creations. Now in her mid twenties, she tells me how she first got into paganism when she went on a camp-out when she was twenty. "There were ten of us and we formed a coven," she says and hands me a yellow flyer advertising their next retreat. I notice that the coven has a Web site. "We all initiated each other one night by making up rituals. We were outside and we drew a circle and blessed each person we were initiating and then branded each other with our coven's secret sign.

"The people I met on my first camp-out, the people who are now in my coven, are my spiritual family, my support network, my best friends. We still get together on all the high holidays and perform rituals." Even Karin's husband is someone she met through her coven. "He was dating somebody else but one Halloween before I went to a witches' ball I lit a bunch of candles in my bathtub and then went out. That night he kissed me for the first time. It was all because of my love spell."

I see Julie—the girl who dressed up like a Catholic school girl for Halloween—at the Eostar (Spring Equinox) Ritual held in Enchantment's backyard to celebrate the arrival of spring. Actually, I don't see her at first because she's playing the part of Spring and is tied up in the chains of winter; that is, she's been bound to a chair with a rope and a cloth over her head. When we have drawn a circle and stomped on the ground in an attempt to wake up Spring, and have sung a song that includes the verse "All sleeping seeds She wakens / The rainbow is her token, / Now Winter's power is taken, / In love all chains are broken" the cloth over her head is removed and the Dark Maiden's identity is revealed.

To symbolize her return from the Dead (i.e., winter), Julie is untied from the chair. Everyone is now chanting "change us, touch us, touch us, change us." Outfitted in a pink and white dress, Julie stands and the cloth is removed from her head. It's nothing like the transformation from girl to woman one would expect with the symbolic awakening of spring. In fact, without her witch's clothing she looks as young and innocent as the stuffed animal she cradles in her arms: a little lamb.

And even Julie seems to be a little lost without her black shrouds. As refreshments and food are served and shared, others in the grove approach Julie and commend her on enduring being tied down for so long—the ritual, after all, lasted more than an hour.

"Oh, that wasn't the worst part of it at all," Julie says and pauses to take a bite of a brownie that's been blessed on the altar. "The worst part of the whole thing was having to wear pastels."

I'm just about to chalk up Wicca to a color you don or a spell you cast when I see Julie being hugged by Joe and Jezebel, the leaders of the grove whom Julie calls her Craft daddy and her Craft mommy.

I watch as Julie and her Craft family dance and laugh and talk, and I remember what Julie told me about Wicca giving her a community, how it gives her *something* to believe in.

Wicca may turn out to be just a phase she's going through, but, for now, she's in her element.

CHAPTER SIX

Love Recipe[1]: *Young Brides*

INGREDIENTS:
  2 Hearts Full of Love

In Las Vegas, land of twenty-four-hour wedding chapels and ever-spinning roulette wheels, not to mention the casinos' never ceasing entertainments—e.g., the Mirage's Vesuvian volcanic eruptions; Treasure Island's outdoor, in-water sea pirate fights; and Circus Circus's, well, circus acts—the only tourist site that seems to follow a clock is the Clark County courthouse. This is where the marriage license bureau is located and where all couples who want to get married in Las Vegas have to go first to get their marriage license, which they can do between the hours of 8:00 A.M. until midnight, Monday through Thursday, and any time between 8:00 A.M. Friday and midnight Sunday.

---

[1]The love recipe is by Charolette Richards, owner of the popular Little White Chapel in Las Vegas Nevada, and is given out on heart-shaped cards to all couples marrying at the chapel. What is one to do with the ingredients (listed here over the course of the following pages)? Richards' instructions: "Stir daily with Happiness, Humor and Patience. Serve with Warmth and Compassion, Respect and Loyalty." Yield? I suppose one happy marriage.

I'm outside the courthouse at eight in the morning on Friday, the Fourth of July, when the doors unlock for the weekly sixty-four-hour marathon session. Over the course of this weekend the bureau will issue 1,914 marriage licenses, making it one of the courthouse's busiest holidays of the year. Other popular times to tie the knot in Vegas are Thanksgiving and New Year's—because this is when couples often have time off from work—and, of course, Valentine's Day.

Unlike the casinos, which, in addition to not having clocks, lack windows and have tinted doors in order to keep you unaware and inside, pulling the arms of slot machines and showing hands, the courthouse's marriage license bureau seems designed to keep visitors out. For starters, the doors are tacked with different colored signs, all bearing warnings.

BLACK SIGN: No Smoking
REDDISH-BROWN SIGN: Stop: Wheelchair Use Only
YELLOW SIGN: Caution: Automatic Door
RED SIGN: Attention: All Weapons Subject to
    Confiscation Beyond This Point

Inside the entranceway is a security checkpoint and two guards, one intimidatingly tall, the other intimidatingly wide. The job responsibilities of a security guard, the skinny one informs me, include chasing away the homeless ("a lot of people come here from other states and aren't used to seeing homeless so they start panicking," he says), making sure nobody cuts in line ("when people've been waiting in line for hours and somebody cuts in front of them, they get pretty upset"), and asking fighting in-laws of young couples to take their disagreements across the street.

Despite all the warnings, security, transients, escortment off the premises, waiting, and premature marital drama, it is unsurprisingly quick and easy to get a marriage license in Las Vegas. No blood test is required, nor is there a waiting period. These are the only rules: Both parties must appear in person at the courthouse with some form of identification and, on an application, state their dates and states of birth, their parents' names, and the "number of this marriage (1st, 2nd, etc.)." Any potential bride or groom who's between sixteen and eighteen needs to have notarized written consent from at least one parent, and couples between fourteen and sixteen can get a license only if they have a court order. A court order costs about $500 in attorney fees, and there has to be a good reason for the couple to get married. Most often the good reason is pregnancy.

2 Cups of Joy

The first young couple to get their marriage license on the Fourth of July has brought an entourage of friends with them from Los Angeles. When the couple emerges from the courthouse, their elaborately tattooed friends surround them the way mobs of Gypsy children spring upon unsuspecting travelers in Italy. Perhaps they think they can steal some of the love. "What took so long?" one of the girls asks. The couple is holding hands, or rather, Rob's holding Elena's ring-finger hand. Hard. She's wearing denim shorts and he's chewing gum and they look even younger than their twenty years. If you didn't know better and if they weren't outside the courthouse, you'd think her ring a gag, a bauble from a gumball machine.

But Rob and Elena have been together for four years and they're determined to make their marriage different from their parents'—both sets of whom are divorced. "I hope that our marriage will be different because we'll stay together," Elena says. She doesn't know, exactly, what she's going to do to ensure they stay together, but she knows what she's not going to do: She's *not* going to drink; she's *not* going to bitch.

When I ask where they're having the ceremony, however, the bride-to-be tosses her black hair back with her free hand and says, "We're getting married at the same chapel both our parents did." She doesn't question whether this makes for an inauspicious beginning, but rather relays this to me in a serious voice that says, "We are keeping up tradition," and with no sense of irony she is priding herself in following the same footsteps as both her parents and her in-laws, whose failed marriages she has derided.

Elena hopes that, unlike her parents' marriage, hers will "work out." But like other young brides in Vegas who entertain the same dream, Elena has to imitate her parents (i.e., *get* married) in order to distinguish her marriage from theirs.

Happy Young Couple Number 4 is just off the plane from Detroit. "The first thing I wanted to do when we landed was get married so we came straight from the airport here," says nineteen-year-old Tanya. She's bleached blond and wearing a lime green tank top that's cut to show off her tanned, flat belly, her navel pierced with a gold ring. She looks like a cheerleader who's had a somewhat tough life, like the new girl at school everyone's curious about, but no one makes the effort to really get to know; after all, it probably won't be long before she moves on again.

Her fiancé, Mike, is wearing a Michigan basketball shirt, gold Nike logo earrings in both ears, and a Nike pendant on a gold necklace. He is older, twenty-eight, and looks at Tanya as though stunned into a silent paralysis by his own luck. After a few minutes of conversation I realize that Mike is, in fact, virtually speechless, and he defers to Tanya for all decision-making and information dissemination.

"Our marriage is going to be different from my parents' because they got divorced and we're going to stay together," Tanya says. Her eyebrows are gone and where they should be are two dark penciled substitutes, lines that are drawn straight across. The severity of her eyebrows accentuates her matter-of-fact tone.

I ask Mike how he feels about Tanya getting married so young. "It's cool," he says, and shrugs.

When I have a few minutes alone with Tanya I ask about the youth factor.

"My mother got married young and that ended bad, so she's not that supportive of the whole thing. I never thought I'd be getting married young, but I met Mike and . . ." Her voice trails off.

"And you fell in love?" I say.

"Well, I wanted to get married."

When, I think, will she wake up and realize that like Tatiana in A *Midsummer Night's Dream*, she's fallen for Bottom? And then it hits me. Tanya's marrying not out of love, but what she hopes will be love. She doesn't want to be awakened; for her, marriage is an initiation into the American family, into the American dream. Like many other young brides, she wants to be more successful than her parents were in many areas, but most prominently in love.

Even before encountering the warnings posted on the courthouse doors, even before the security guards, young brides coming to Vegas to marry have had a lot to scare them off—namely, their parents' marriages. After talking with young brides about their parents' marriages, all unhappy marriages begin to sound the same.

So why are these young brides I'm meeting, almost all of whom come from divorced families, so eager to tie the knot? According to the census bureau, in 1997, the median age at first marriage for women was 25 (for men, 26.8). In 1987 the median age at first marriage for women was 23.6 (for men, 25.8). And ten years before that, in 1977, the numbers were 21.6 for women (24 for men). In fact, the median age at first marriage has been rising since 1956, when it was 20.1 for women, 22.5 for men. What these numbers mean is that on the whole, women who were marrying at twenty or twenty-one in the past are now waiting longer and that these young brides I'm meeting in Vegas are not the norm.

When I talk to Andrew Cherlin, a professor of sociology at Johns Hopkins University who has studied the effects of parental divorce on children, he tells me that he and his colleagues found that children of divorced parents, due to friction with their parents, are more likely than not to have a first partnership at a younger age and to leave home and live with that partner.

As I stand outside the courthouse with these young brides-to-be I'm struck by the urgency with which these women are seeking the stable family structures they didn't have growing up. Living with someone is not enough; they want to make what they have official. Of course, there are many ways in which a girl's parents' divorce may affect her, but one is certainly to propel her to the altar quickly— and perhaps prematurely. Indeed, Cherlin tells me that teenage marriages are more likely to end in divorce. (While the national census bureau has no current reports about the current rate of divorce among American teenagers, the bureau estimates that divorce will be the end result of almost fifty percent of all marriages today.)

What is the difference between the young men and the women getting hitched in Vegas? To make a totally reductive but perhaps not unfair observation, it seems that while most young grooms marry in order to gain a wife, most of the young brides marry to secure a life.

2 Minds Full of Tenderness

While some of the older soon-to-be-brides at the courthouse act like gamblers about to bet all their chips on something that's not even a sure thing—one forty-something-year-old exiting her limousine and apparently rejoicing in the adrenaline and the craziness of marrying a man she's just met, shouts, "I'm going for it"—the younger brides do no such thing. More likely than not they're marrying their long-term boyfriend, and they look as though if they had one wish at that moment, it would be that their mothers were around to hold their hands.

Perhaps the twenty-one-and-younger brides, who make up a quarter of the brides-in-waiting, seem to take marriage more seriously than the older ones because having grown up in the midst of divorce they know the stakes are high. In the absence of a mother's hand, they find comfort, and almost seek refuge, in Las Vegas's prepackaged love assurances. Wedding packages on the Strip range from the Graceland Wedding Chapel's $50 basic fee for use of chapel, witness, and music (Elvis impersonators are available to entertain for

$120 extra) to the Little White Chapel's Joan Collins Special, which costs $499 and includes use of the chapel, a candlelight ceremony, music, six 8x10s, six 5x7s, six wallet photographs, two bridal bouquets, two corsages, four boutonnieres, a bride's garter, champagne glasses, a lithographed marriage certificate, a video recording, a wedding cake (only included if it's reserved at least 24 hours in advance), and an etched marriage scroll. And, of course, the love recipe.

The wedding packages and the chapels themselves offer the comfort of a recipe for love, and the illusion that such a recipe exists. "You're doing good," the packages and chapels assure these young couples. "If you want everlasting love, you've come to the right place."

The Little White Chapel is one of the most frequented of the fifty wedding chapels on the Strip. A popular backdrop for wedding photos is the sign outside the chapel boasting that both Joan Collins (hence the Joan Collins Special package) and Michael Jordan were married there. The Michael Jordan wedding package, which comes with a garter for both the bride and the groom, and costs $389, making it the second most expensive package after the Joan Collins Special, is the most popular of all the packages. That Joan Collins's and Michael Jordan's love lives are something people want to emulate isn't even questioned here; in Las Vegas churches, it's not religion but celebrity that's the opiate of the people.

One day I watch a nervous bride waiting to be married by one of the Little White Chapel's three ministers. She is twenty years old and, with trembling fingers, she holds a bouquet of plastic flowers her sister arranged for her back home in Philadelphia. When it's her turn the minister tries to calm her down.

"How long is the ceremony?" the white-gowned Caitlin asks. She looks as though her decision of whether or not to get married is predicated upon the minister's response.

"How long do you want it to be?" the minister says. "I can go on for hours." Miraculously, he manages to cajole a smile out of the bride. "I'll do the richer and poorer, all that stuff."

Caitlin's parents' marriage ended in divorce she tells the minister, and she has mixed feelings about the whole thing. Her husband, a blond boy with a long forehead and large hands, rubs the bare part of her back revealed by the U of her scoop-backed dress, and she pulls away. Tears threaten to gush, until she notices all the photographs on one wall of the "waiting room" outside the chapel.

"Is that Ricki Lake?" she asks, focusing on one of the many photographs. She looks as though she might drop her bouquet right then and there.

"Yes, Ricki Lake got married here," the minister says proudly.

Another young bride-in-waiting who's wearing a short black leather skirt hears him and approaches the wall. "Ricki Lake got married here!?" she says, unintentionally summoning almost every young woman in the room to examine the picture.

"Yes, there in the white hat," the minister says to all the inquiring eyes. Realizing he has a captive audience he continues, "And there's the woman from *Falcon Crest*." He points to another picture and all the women (there are now five of them, all under twenty-five) ooh and aah, although it's unlikely any of them know her name or remember *Falcon Crest* as more than a show that featured wealth and drama and was on late at night. This association, however, and the fact that the woman from *Falcon Crest* got married at this very chapel, where they're going to marry, is enough to impress them.

"And here's Mickey Rooney and here's Mickey Rooney and here's Mickey Rooney," the minister says, pointing to three different photographs of Mickey Rooney, all with different wives. With each marriage, Rooney looks progressively older, his wives increasingly younger.

"Oh my God," says the woman in the black leather skirt. "He sure does like this chapel!"

All the young brides' fears seem assuaged by the fact that someone keeps coming back to the chapel. It doesn't seem to register with them that the reason Mickey Rooney keeps coming back for more is because his marriages never last.

But this is Las Vegas, where names mean a lot (where even "the woman from *Falcon Crest*" is a name) and numbers mean even more. Pacified and assured at last by the fame and fortune that has gone down the aisle before her, plastic-bouquet-holding Caitlin, still staring at the wall of fame, says, "I think I'm ready now."

2 Heaping Cups of Kindness

"About two-thirds of the weddings I do are couples who are between eighteen and twenty-five," says Charolette Richards, who started the Little White Chapel over thirty-nine years ago, making it the oldest wedding chapel in Las Vegas.

A mother of four and a grandmother of six, Richards is serious about the role she takes as a sort of den mother to the young couples she marries. Richards, a former beauty pageant winner with blue eyes and shoulder-length strawberry-blond hair, doesn't look her age. She married when she was eighteen, and her marriage lasted eighteen years until her husband died, at which point she took over their wedding business to support herself and her family. Perhaps because her own marriage was full of ups and downs and "wasn't exactly a bowl full of roses," but still full of love, she has plenty of advice for young couples. She tells them to work through their problems, to seek counseling if they need it, and to work together in a godly manner. "Young couples today don't have a knowledge of God," she says.

"The one change I've noticed is that although there are more young couples getting married today, and most of them are even younger than the young couples that were getting married ten, twenty, thirty years ago, is usually they've been together longer," Richards tells me. "Ninety-five percent of the young couples have been together three to six months, or three to six years even. Today, a lot more young couples live together, and experience their feelings before marrying. Very seldom do they get married after just having met."

By her estimation, in the past thirty-nine years over a million weddings have taken place in one of her three Las Vegas chapels:

the Little White Chapel, the Chapel by the Courthouse (so-called because it's by the courthouse), and We've Only Just Begun, the first of the now many Las Vegas chapels to be located inside a hotel (it's inside the Imperial Palace Hotel). Currently, she's constructing a wedding center that will offer everything from manicures to ministers—a trip to the courthouse is the only other stop couples will have to make before tying the knot.

"Whether they come from broken homes or good homes, for a lot of these young couples, marriage is a way of starting their lives," Richards tells me in a confiding manner. "The problem is that they haven't been taught what love really is, they haven't been disciplined. For the most part they've been neglected. I think this is because there are more elements today that create this neglect on the parents' part—there's divorce, and I think people today are more into themselves than they ever were before. Plus, the children of young mothers who were married twenty years ago are now getting married because they don't know better." Richards shakes her head. "We have to set an example for our children."

4 Arms of Gentleness

Some of the parents do chaperone their children to the wedding chapel, yet it's unclear what kind of example, exactly, they're setting.

Vicki and Ray live a two-hour drive from Vegas, and Ray's father and his girlfriend have come to the courthouse with them. Ray is sixteen and Vicki is seventeen, but, largely due to the enormous hickey on her neck—the kind of hickey you give/get when you're first discovering them—and his baseball hat, they look even younger than they are. They already live together and want to keep living together and growing closer, so they've decided to get married and start a family.

While I'm talking with Ray and Vicki, Ray's father comes up to them—his girlfriend's waiting in the car—and says, "Hey, Ray, got a smoke?"

"It's my last one," Ray says, flipping open the box of his nearly empty Camel pack as evidence. The father deliberates, and decides to let his son have the cigarette. It is, after all, his wedding day and he might need it.

"Hey, Vicki, got any money?" Ray's father asks.

"No, I don't get my paycheck till tomorrow," she says.

Ray's father slides his hands into the empty pockets of his dark blue jeans. "Well," he says, "if it's okay by you, we're going to skip the chapel and see you guys tomorrow."

"Okay," Ray says, completely unfazed that his father isn't coming to the wedding. His father pats him on the back and walks back to the voice of his girlfriend, beckoning him from the car. There's a drunken meander to his bowlegged gait.

I ask Ray why his father got married to his mother, from whom he is now divorced. "Necessity," Ray says.

"With my parents," Vicki adds, "well, can you say 'accident'? Ray and I are different—we're getting married for love."

Their ceremony is going to be at the chapel across the street from their motel. And for the honeymoon? "We're going back to the motel and scrog," Vicki says. She lifts her head and smiles up at Ray, flashing another love bite, this one under her chin. "Hey, it's honest," she says and shrugs.

2 Big Hearts Full of Forgiveness

It's a strange occurrence, as an interviewer, to have the tables turned on you, but this is what happens to me on more than a few unsolicited occasions while talking to young brides. For them, you see, love is a conversation starter.

"Are you married?" asks a bride whose first marriage was annulled (she was eighteen and had youthful ideas about wanting to move to

Australia and work and so she married for her green card—"what a mess," she says now).

"What about you? Are you married?" asks a sixteen-year-old, whose mother is outside the courthouse collecting cans to cash in for their recycling value.

"Married?" says a girl from Texas, who's been fighting with her boyfriend in the line for her license. She's wearing a robin's egg blue dress with upside-down butterflies all over it, fluttering toward the hem, and I can't help thinking that, in marriage, she's hoping for a metamorphosis of sorts.

Inevitably, "How old are you?" is their next question. And no one quite knows how to respond when I tell them I'm twenty-five. The bride from Texas checks my naked ring finger (perhaps to make sure I'm not kidding) and then, in a Southern drawl says, "Well, you have really pretty hair." Some sort of consolation, she feels, is due.

In the eyes of these young brides, at twenty-five I am a spinster. To them, the only possible conclusion is that I have been unlucky in love. Yet being in Las Vegas, I have never felt so fortunate to *not* be married. This has less to do with talking with young brides, than who I am with in Las Vegas and why.

Understand: I'm here with Ex Boyfriend, who I dated in my late teens. When Ex Boyfriend and I were together marriage didn't seem inconceivable, but now it's hard to remember why we lasted more than a few weeks. EB and I broke up years ago (there was the lying, the cheating, etc.), but agreed to meet up in Vegas because he wanted to gamble, I wanted to talk to young brides, and in that un-thought-out way that precedes many bad ideas, we thought it would be fun.

After only a few hours together we decide to each go our own ways (there's a reason we broke up) and spend the remainder of our time in Vegas successfully avoiding each other by using the absence of clocks as an excuse. "I lost track of time," we say to each other when we fail to show up at the agreed upon hour for breakfast, lunch, dinner, or blackjack. (We chastely share a single room with two double beds.)

EB drinks himself and all the girls he buys Fauvist-colored drinks for into a costly oblivion, and goes back to these girls' hotel rooms, and even asks me for suggestions on how to extricate himself from the myriad entanglements he's managed to weave about him in an impressively small span of time—the fact that he's been drinking while taking medication may have led to: his bar bill at the poolside Cabana Bar; his incessant flirtation and subsequent hook-up with Jodie, a girl in a black dress at the craps table; and his "altercation" with Jodie's boyfriend. Not to mention that he's writing out checks to me in exchange for cash because he's already succeeded in withdrawing the maximum amount he can withdraw per day from the cash machine (which, in Vegas, is a lot, and this he has done every day we've been in Vegas) in a (futile) attempt to win back his losses.

And all the while, I think, Thank God we don't have a joint bank account, thank God we don't have any promises to each other, thank God we're not married. Because, can you just imagine . . .

2 Cups of Friendship

Shane and Thea are twenty and nineteen, the same ages EB and I were when we started dating. I meet them outside the courthouse one day and Shane explains to me why they're getting married. "She completes me," he says, quoting Tom Cruise's line from *Jerry Maguire*. It's supposed to be a parody, but I get the feeling he doesn't have a better answer.

Both from Whittier, California, Shane and Thea take a lot of their clues about life—including love—from movies and TV. Even the way Thea dresses is straight off of MTV—with bottle-blond short hair that's cut to reveal an ear full of earrings and a black dress with large orange flowers, she could be anyone from Lilith Fair. Shane's hair is also dyed—it's red—and he has crooked teeth that make him look at once goofy and lovable: a clown.

They've only been dating for a month, but they've been friends for seven years, ever since they met at a roller rink where she was working. Proud of this retro detail, they make much of the rink—it is, after all, like something off an old TV show.

"My parents are divorced. So it's pretty scary to be getting married," Thea says. "But I think we can manage, we're pretty cool friends. I mean, there's always been that feeling, but we never acted on it."

"We tell each other everything," Shane adds, "no matter what."

They don't, however, tell their parents everything.

"We didn't tell our parents we were getting married because we didn't want all the questions like, 'How are you going to support yourself,'" Shane says.

Perhaps it's not the questions themselves they were avoiding, but the fact that they lack a response—Shane works in a warehouse and Thea works part-time and is going to school.

"I think my mother might be a little upset because she wanted me to finish school first," Thea says, and looks at the ground, at nothing in particular.

"I think it will be okay," Shane says, looking at Thea, who's still looking at nothing. Then he turns to me and offers reasons for his optimism. "At my birthday party her mother gave me a shirt, and I'm all, 'I'm going to wear this to the wedding,' and she's all, 'What wedding?' I'm all, 'I'm going to marry your daughter this weekend.' And she's all, 'Fuck you.' And then two seconds later she turned to her boyfriend and said, 'Hey, meet my son-in-law.' So that's how it will be. It will be, 'What?' and then it will be, 'Okay, I love you.'"

They're going to get married at the Little White Chapel's drive-through.

When I ask why, Thea says, "Because we saw it on TV and we thought it would be cool. It was on a news show," she adds, as though this gives it credence, makes it officially a place where couples who will be together forever get married.

"Which news show?" I ask.

"Um, I think *Hard Copy*."

• • •

1 Lifetime Full of Togetherness

I ended up going to Shane and Thea's wedding, if you can call standing in the parking lot and watching their car go through a drive-through attending a ceremony. They invited me to come because their friends who were supposed to come to Vegas to watch them get married "flaked out in the last minute."

The drive-through is on the side of the Little White Chapel, and how it works is you drive up and ring a bell and, for $25, the window opens and a head slides out and marries you. It's the only drive-through chapel in Vegas, and Charolette Richards told me she got the idea because she wanted to make getting married easier for the handicapped, and for those with lots of small children who didn't want to have to spend a lot of money getting them all gussied up. About ten percent of the marriages at the Little White Chapel are performed at the drive-through, and that's not just cars—people come through on Rollerblades, bikes, and even horse and buggies. It's the young people in particular who seem to favor the drive-through because, not unlike meeting your spouse at a roller rink, it's "cool."

While waiting outside the flower shop for Shane and Thea's turn—the flower shop continuously plays "Going to the Chapel"— I watch two couples in a red Suzuki with California plates drive up to the window. The strange thing about the double wedding is that both grooms are in the front seat while their brides are in the back. When it comes time to kiss the brides, the grooms turn around, straining their necks, and end up getting pecks near their sideburns.

In their red, bumper-dented mideighties Mustang convertible, Shane and Thea are the next to pull up. He is, in fact, wearing the shirt Thea's mother gave him for his twentieth birthday the week before. Thea's wearing an orange scarf around her head, as though to keep her hair back, but the truth is that her hair is so short that the vintage scarf is a stylish affectation. Her dark sunglasses cover so much of her small face that she looks like a girl who's swiped her mother's shades for a game of dress-up.

The whole process takes longer than driving up to get a hamburger. Unlike at a fast food drive-through, at a chapel drive-through you actually turn off your engine. Shane busies himself with the forms and smiles at Thea and at one point even runs one of his thick fingers all the way down her cheek, and then down the side of her body.

When they've been officially married they kiss a long kiss and then, because there's a car behind them, Shane starts the engine. Suddenly, they're confronted with the reality of the situation: Although the drive-through is ostensibly supposed to save you time, they're not in much of a rush. They pull up so the car behind them can take their spot at the drive-through's window. They pause. The rear blinker signals that they're about to turn left. Then right. Then the signal is turned off. They look at each other. Shane kisses Thea. Thea kisses Shane. And then Thea takes the marriage certificate from her husband and, through the dark lenses of her big sunglasses, stares at it for a long, long time, studying it as though it's the most recent clue on a scavenger hunt for love, a clue that will direct them where to go next.

Burning Man

I am standing in the middle of a Nevada desert on the Sunday of Labor Day weekend amid fifteen thousand people—many of them naked—who dance, drum, and cheer as a forty-foot neon-tube-outlined wooden effigy of a man is set on fire. Some people shake rubber chickens at the Man, others throw women's lace underwear in his direction, one guy places a pizza box at the Man's feet, or rather, where his feet would be if he had extremities, and almost everyone chants "Burn him!" The crowd's passion (what has this expressionless stick figure ever done to them?) and energy (this night is the culmination of what for some has been a four-day orgy of drinking, drugging, and dancing) is unlike anything I have ever witnessed (and during the past few days I've seen *plenty*). It was to understand what inspired this passion, energy, and growing devotion to a ritual whose meaning is unstated and open to personal inter-pretation—a ritual with no determined significance?—that I ven-tured to the 1997 Burning Man festival.

Many things about the annual Burning Man have changed in the dozen years since its inception on a San Francisco beach—the time (originally it took place in June in honor of the summer solstice); the place (it's moved from the aforementioned beach to the Nevada desert); the size of the effigy (the Man has grown from eight feet to forty); the length of the event (instead of a one-night festivity, it now spans the course of an entire long weekend, plus); and the number of attendees (the count's gone from twenty to fifteen thousand). One thing that has not altered is that Burning Man-ners—devotees who make the trek from around the world every year to watch the Man burn—maintain that the ritual provides their lives with something missing from their everyday existence: community.

Having grown up in San Francisco, I'd been hearing about Burning Man for years. It always had an aura of the primitive. I was intrigued by the ritual of it, by the focus on fire, by the fact that no matter how many people I asked I could never get a very clear idea of what it was all about. I'd never seriously considered making the trek to the desert myself, but the summer of 1997 was different. My research for this book had led me to discussions with young women about their experiences belonging to a group and I had begun to get a sense of the needs which compel so many people to be a part of some community. As for myself, I was unaffiliated and increasingly disconnected, more so because of my discovery that everyone else seemed to be affiliated/connected/communitized. Even my friends. Unlike them, I didn't belong to a church/synagogue/mosque, a softball team, the Junior League, a yoga institute, a reading circle, a tennis ladder, a CD club, the Yeats society, or AA.

As I began to acknowledge my status as a non–community member, Burning Man took on a new appeal. I imagined that if the world was tilted on its axis, everyone who wasn't tied down to a community would slide into Black Rock City, as Burning Man-ners have christened their Arcadia. And so I went to Burning Man to investigate if, after all, there was a place for people like me; I went to Burning Man wondering if something totally transformative would occur and I would come away from it with a new Sense of Belonging.

To get to Burning Man I flew from New York to San Francisco and met up with my younger sister, Vanessa. Vanessa is a psychology major at Berkeley whose motivations for going to Burning Man were totally different from mine. Initially, I was surprised she wanted to accompany me on my trek. Her reasons? "I'm reading Freud's *Civilization and Its Discontents* and I was thinking that, well, isn't Burning Man a civilization created by discontents?

"Plus," she continued, "these really cute guys who sit behind me in Developmental Psychopathology were talking about how they're going. I'm *there.*"

So on the Thursday evening before Labor Day weekend, our trunk packed with camping equipment and our glove compartment stuffed with maps, directions, and various Burning Man "survival guide" tips we've been sent in the mail along with our tickets, we head off from San Francisco for Black Rock City. After driving East for four hours we stop at a Sak 'N Save on the outskirts of Reno.

We've just begun filling up our cart with the two gallons of water per person per day recommended in the Burning Man survival kit when some Teva-footed and Patagonia-clad people in Aisle 4 who are volleyballing a Sak 'N Save pink beach ball between them say, "Burning Man?"

"How'd you know?" I ask.

Green Patagonia spikes the ball and then nods at our water jug–stacked shopping cart. Our cart is full, but when we join the checkout line it appears we're a bit understocked for Burning Man. Like Vanessa and me, the couple in front of us has a shopping cart with water bottles practically toppling out. Unlike us, they have another cart packed with Sam Adams's, Jack Daniels, Smirnoff, Marlboros, and Advil. The group of guys in back of us have two carts, both loaded with beer. On the bottom rack of one cart are several ice blocks the size of laundry bags. On the bottom rack of the other sit three inflated pink beach balls. I feel as though I've got a big sticker on my butt that says "Burning Man Virgin."

The checkout boy is pimply and nervous, Central Casting's nightshift supermarket boy. He asks where we're heading and tells us that he only knows about Burning Man because one time he and his friends were driving through the desert and they came across a forty-foot man. "We didn't know what the heck was going on," he says. "It was really weird."

It's well after midnight and we've been driving in the dark in what looks like post-apocalyptic terrain—it's just been us and the tumbleweed—when suddenly an illuminated metropolis rises up before us like the Emerald City in *The Wizard of Oz*. I had imagined Black Rock City would look like a very big campground—a bunch of tents, portable stoves, and flashlights—but instead trailers, RVs with satellite dishes, and rotating searchlights abound. And there, in the center of it all, stands a neon blue figure in the shape of a man. We've arrived.

Halfway down the road that leads to the start of the city, a hare-lipped woman with a coal miner's light on her head waves us down, takes our tickets, and hands us a map of Black Rock City. Like a real city, Black Rock has streets, a city center, and suburbs. A surveyor designs the city around the focal point so that the streets are essentially concentric circles around the Man—one circle outside another, like a dart board. Acting as though we are on a quest for the heart of darkness, we head straight downtown, toward the Man himself.

"To describe Burning Man, the great upwelling of creative energy that occurs in the Nevada desert every year preceding Labor Day, is like describing the abundance—the sheer, prodigal, and superfluous fertility—of Nature itself," reads the first paragraph of a pamphlet about Burning Man that I received in the mail with my tickets and survival guide. But when we arrive at an empty campsite in downtown Black Rock—we're directed there by a drunk guy on a bike with a painted-blue face—we step out of the car and into pounding techno music. This is a rather unusual Nature. The only sense in which I'm experiencing a return to primitive conditions is that I feel like I'm in the epicenter of a fifteen thousand-person all-night Bacchanalia.

Vanessa and I have traveled to villages without electricity in Third World countries, we've gone alone to places where guidebooks strongly advise against women traveling without male accompaniment, and yet upon our arrival at Burning Man, I feel as though we've just arrived in the center of Hieronymus Bosch's *Garden of Earthly Delights*. Various camps have improvised a battle of the bands (that is, a struggle to assert the superiority of their taste in music merely by playing it at the highest decibel), and the resulting cacophony makes the Tower of Babel seem positively peaceful. Everyone is in various states of both undress and advancement in their drug enhancement/impairment programs, and there appears to exist an inverse relationship between the former and the latter: The greater the drug intake, the scarcer the clothing. To call the scene before us Felliniesque would be an understatement. Frankly, we're scared. It's one o'clock and we decide to wait until the sun's out to set up our tent; we lower the car seats, lock the car doors, and sleep.

When I wake up in the car the next morning the first person I see through the window is a naked woman. What's more bizarre than waking up to nude strangers is how quickly one becomes accustomed to seeing nude strangers. After Vanessa and I set up the tent, we start walking around Black Rock City and it takes less than an hour for me to become fairly oblivious to who's naked and who's not. Sometimes I just notice people's body pierces (seeing naked people makes you realize how many places there are on your body for unusual pierces). Neither gender nor body type prevents people from showing all they've got, and I find it interesting to see how many places there are on a body for fat deposits—I even see a guy with a fat spine. From a distance, I often think people are clothed, only to discover as we approach that they've just painted clothes on—bikini tops, shorts, shirts, even G-string underwear.

The male/female ratio at Burning Man is roughly even, and the average age of the attendees is twenty-seven, with most being between eighteen and forty. There is, of course, the occasional couple in their sixties, and surprisingly, a lot of kids. The kids spend most of their time doing roughly what the adults are doing—riding around on their bikes, dancing, talking to people—but unlike in Society, it's the adults who are naked and the kids who are clothed. One eight-year-old girl we meet named Marjorie has a banana bike with her, but she tells us she's only allowed to ride it "around the block." "I keep an eye on my dad's Camp Barbie," she says. "You want to see?"

Like a carnival with lots of booths, Burning Man comprises camps, which many people have spent a lot of money and time preparing. We follow Marjorie to her father's camp, a display of about thirty Barbies, all of which are mutated in some way. "I helped him make that one," she says, and she points to a hirsute Barbie. "I glued the hair on its back." This, I think, is what separates a Burning Man kid from a normal cute blond suburban girl on a banana bike: she derives great pleasure and a humongous missing-a-couple-of-teeth smile from deforming dolls, and she refers to Barbie as an "it."

In some ways Burning Man is made for kids, what with the mud and the games and the bikes. But in other respects it seems entirely wrong because a large percentage of the camps have sex-based themes. There's a confession booth for telling stories about something that made you laugh in bed, and some women walk around on stilts wearing to-the-knee dildos and shouting "Show us your cocks" to all the men in the vicinity.

We pass a camp with a sign saying "Leave your shoes at the door and come in and wash your souls." Another camp features scantily clad women who ask if you want to get laid, and regardless of your response, bedeck you with plastic leis. "What's up with the puns?" Vanessa says, as a woman walks by us with a big plastic hammer and says "Get hammered" to everyone she encounters, before bopping them on the head.

Puns, in fact, abound at Burning Man—perhaps because they provide an easy entrée into interaction; they make it seem as though everyone's privy to the same punchline of a joke. "This is so lame," Vanessa says. "Everything is not funny. Okay, maybe the first time, but after the hundredth time—no, scratch that—after the fifth time it's just pathetic. Who are these people?" She tells me she wants to go back to our camp and read; I agree to meet her there at three o'clock. I want to yell something protective after her like "Don't talk to any weirdos," but I refrain because at Burning Man this is essentially impossible.

Sisterless, I am left standing in front of Temps Perdu, the big cafe in the center of Black Rock City. The cafe has haystacks and tables and, improbably, an espresso machine. Stretched across the width of the cafe's partial roof is a banner that reads, "No Spectators."

The "no spectators" refrain is a popular one at Burning man. According to Larry Harvey, one of the event's founding fathers, Burning Man is an alternative to the TV-watching culture of America. Therefore, everyone should be a participant. Participants are good, spectators bad, and the distinction between the two groups is not insubstantial. Spectators suffer a fate worse than that of high school outcasts: They're taunted, sneered at, and abused by the "in" crowd, i.e., the elite, the participants. The media are considered the biggest spectators around and it's par for the course that Burning Man participants clank bells into news reporters' microphones and/ or squirt water directly at their video camera lenses while announcing, "This is Media Interference."

Some participants have spent a good part of the year conceiving an idea for a theme camp and saving up for U-Hauls and RVs to transport all the necessary theme-camp furnishings to Burning Man. This type of participant makes up about 50 percent of Burning Man's population; another 25 percent is made up of the sort of participants who run around on acid, Ecstasy, 'shrooms or pot, taking part in (those doing pot or Ecstasy) or freaking out about (those on acid and 'shrooms) the aforementioned participants' creations.

Despite all the professed animosity toward their kind, the remaining 25 percent of Black Rock City is made up of spectators. Even the people sitting on haystacks underneath the "No Spectators" banner are spectators. Sipping cappuccinos from the cafe, they read the Black Rock Gazette (Burning Man's daily newspaper) while listening to 99.5 (Burning Man's radio station). Their primary pastime, however, seems to be sitting and watching all the weird people who pass by. Some spectators even film the participants with video cameras so that they can watch them on TV when they get home.

The general consensus is that being a participant is the only way to fully experience Burning Man. Although I haven't brought anything to share with anyone else, my desire to be initiated into the world of participants—and thereby discover a Sense of Belonging—leads me to the Sunscreen Camp. To keep the heat of the desert away from pale skin, some opt for parasols, others for strategically placed Band-Aids. Most go the sunscreen route, however, and this is one of the reasons the Sunscreen Camp is so popular. The Sunscreen Camp is shaded by a large canopy, and beneath it are two massage tables, a tub of sunscreen, and ten volunteer sunscreeners. The camp's motto, as stated on a large banner, is "Burn the Man, Not Your Body."

Wendy, a storklike woman with bright eyes and prominent ribs who's (only) wearing men's BVDs tells me she started the camp after coming to Burning Man last year and seeing all the burned bodies by the end of the event. "The camp's turning out to be quite popular," Wendy says with pride, as though she's an entrepreneur whose company has just gone public. "We've had constant lines and more than enough volunteers."

A line of eight people are waiting for a massage—among them, a naked man, the naked man's clothed five-year-old son, three naked women, and a couple who just got married the night before beneath the Man. When it's my turn to get sunscreened I lay on my stomach on a table and think, This is all for free! Never would this happen in Society, never would this happen to my friends who frequent spas. Three (three!) volunteer masseuses/sunscreeners get to work on me—one on my right foot, one on my back, and one on my arms.

The guy who's massaging my foot twists it slowly in all sorts of strange directions. I've never really believed foot fetishists existed beyond the personal ads in the *Village Voice*, but this guy makes me wonder. A theatrical set designer from Houston, he tells me that his dream is to one day do the design for the set of *Alice in Wonderland*. "I want to do everything—the set, the mushroom, the costumes," he says as he enthusiastically rubs lotion between my second and third toes. "I saw a production of it last year and the whole thing was wrong. I mean, the guy's vision was so far off it was unbelievable. I've never seen anyone do a good *Alice*. With my vision, I have to do it. No one even pictures Alice the way I do."

"How do you picture her?" I ask.

"In high stiletto heels," he says.

The guy who's doing my back rubs lotion in with one hand and uses the other to draw shapes. For a few minutes I try to decipher whatever code it is I'm sure he's spelling out on my back. I focus hard. If he is communicating some secret message, however, it's DXYBCOZ. I decide he's just trying to confuse me. The back rubber is from L.A., where he organizes raves. He tells me he resents the popular perception that Burning Man is a hippie fest. "Hippies are just trying to relive the summer of sixty-three [sic]. We're here because we're artists. This is an artistic community."

My arms feel like they're being pulled out of their sockets by a computer programmer from Colorado who, like a large percentage of people at Burning Man, found out about the event over the Internet. "I was just surfing the Net and I kept hearing about this big party and it sounded so cool that I had to check it out for myself." He's come alone as, it turns out, have the other sunscreeners. I realize that this is what the Sunscreen Camp is all about. People who spend most of their days in front of a computer can drive a day or two, or however faraway Loneliness is, come to the Sunscreen Camp and talk to and touch real people.

Of course this is true of Burning Man itself. People from around the country, and even from abroad, read about Burning Man on the Internet or find out about it from a *Wired* magazine article from the year before that seems to function as a *Let's Go* guidebook for a lot of these people coming to Burning Man, and simply by showing up and becoming participants can make friends with fifteen thousand people. People who will talk to them, massage them, give them drugs, dance with them.

Like the back rubber/rave organizer, the computer programmer views himself as taking part in an artists' republic. He massages my hands, and at one point locks fingers with me. "It's so important," he tells me while squeezing my hand, "for artists to connect."

As I'm leaving the Sunscreen Camp, a man on a bike with a cart trailing behind him rings the silver bell on his handlebar.

"Do you need a ride?" he asks.

"Sure," I say.

"Where do you need to go?"

There isn't anywhere is particular I need to go. But I've adopted the attitude that if I'm going to find Community I have to participate, experience, etc. I see a Canadian flag on the top of an RV in the distance and decide it's a reasonable ride from where we are to there and as good a place as any so I point toward it and say, "To Canada."

My chauffeur's name is Greg, he's about forty five years old, and his bark-textured face is red and his eyebrows have been bleached white by the sun. This is Greg's fourth Burning Man. He's surprised when I ask him why he keeps coming back, as though there would be any reason why he *wouldn't* come back.

"The people here are great," he says, "and I love camping." I look around at the city of fifteen thousand cramped into the smallest possible quarters and think how this is more like refugee camping.

Before I get into the cart, Greg offers me a prize. I close my eyes and reach into a baseball cap that still feels sweaty around the rim and pull out a sticker that says, "Burning Man '97."

"Cool," I say, and get into the back of the cart where I sit on an upside-down milk crate. Before we take off Greg offers me a water bottle full of beer. The beer is murky and things are floating inside the water bottle so that it looks like an aquarium that hasn't been cleaned for a while.

"It's too hot to drink," I say. Even my desire to experience isn't enough to force me to stomach the concoction.

"Too hot to drink?" He makes a perplexed face and his blond eyebrows become one long mustache on his forehead and his wrinkles as pronounced as the lines of a Dürer woodcut. He takes a swig, then another, and then a third really long one, and then we're off. We travel down the dirt road and pass by naked people on bikes— some dually disclothed on tandem bikes. The dirt rises and the wheels of the cart squeak and Greg pedals furiously. When we arrive at the Canadian flag he's out of breath. His face is redder, his eyebrows whiter.

I get off and thank him.

"Where are you going?"

"I'm not sure yet," I say.

"You mean you had me come all this way and it wasn't even your destination?"

I want to explain to Greg that because I don't know what I'm hoping to find or where, exactly, I think I might find it, I can't give him specific directions. But instead I shrug sheepishly.

"Well, have a good Burning Man," he says as he mounts his bike, looking like he's having second thoughts about liking *all* the people at Burning Man.

I make my way over to a camp that's called House of Doors, which is exactly that: at least forty doors of various shapes, sizes, and colors that have been hinged together. I walk by all the doors and look inside the area that's been created by the circumference of the doors, but there's no one there and not much to do except think, Where'd they get all these doors and how did they get them up here, and did they hinge together here or before they came? So I leave.

Next I go to Camp Boise. The people who set it up are from Idaho (judging by both the name of the camp and the Idaho license plates on their RV). You're supposed to visit these camps and "participate" in whatever's going on, so I sit down on a lawn chair in Camp Boise. But there's no one there—they're probably out checking out other people's camps who are out checking out other people's camps, etc. I wait for a while, nothing much happens, so I leave.

The more I walk around, the more I'm convinced that Burning Man is a physical manifestation of the Internet—essentially, it's a big open space that you can travel around however you choose. Considering that an impressive number of Burning Man-ners find out about the event on the Net or from *Wired* magazine, it makes sense that when given the tabula rasa of the desert, they use it to construct what they know best: real live Web sites. This insight begins to affect my perception of all the theme camps. When I run into people I've met in the line for Sunscreen Camp or hanging out at Cafe Temps Perdu and they ask me where I'm going, in my head I add domains to every response. "I'm going to the trojanhorse.edu" or "I'm headed toward icesculpture.com" or "I'm going to biancassmutshack.org."

Bianca's Smut Shack is supposed to be a house of ill repute, but no one's doing anything that could really give them a bad reputation; in fact, no one's doing much of anything. Bianca has hauled trucks full of ratty futons and mattresses and couches and positioned them under tarps. Everyone hangs out there looking artsy, bad, and heroin chic. It's as though the Smut Shack Slackers have seen too many ads for Diesel Jeans, the ads where it looks like the morning after a party (and at Burning Man, it always is the morning after a party) or that they're trying to be the alternative to the MTV Beach House. Instead of dancing around to music by swimming pools, they're sinking into Chianti-colored velveteen couches and occasionally painting each other's nails hues like jaundice.

In the early afternoon I make my way back to our campsite, orienteering myself by way of various Burning Man landmarks: I turn right at a big U-Haul that says "Come to Minnesota, land of 100,000 lakes," left at a trampoline, and right at a CNN RV. When I get back to our campsite Vanessa's sitting outside on one of our sun chairs in a bikini reading Freud's *Civilization and Its Discontents*. She's found a passage relevant to Burning Man and reads aloud, "Freud called it the contention that what we call our civilization is largely responsible for our misery, and that we should be much happier if we gave it up and returned to primitive conditions."

"What's interesting," she says, peering up at me over her sunglasses, "is that Freud could never check out his theories. I mean, imagine what he would have thought of Burning Man."

Before we can discuss this further, one of our neighbors, who has shoulder-length dark hair and perfectly even teeth, comes over and lurks near our table and chairs. Vanessa closes her thin paperback book with the definitiveness of someone closing a Bible, and we spend the rest of the afternoon getting to know our neighbors.

The word *neighbors* is an understatement because it implies that those camped around us live at a distance, when they're really in our face. The neighbor with the even teeth tells us, "I am a sponge. In real life, I'm an artist, but what I'm doing here is absorbing creativity."

He shows us a poem he once wrote and that he's had printed up on triangular-shaped business cards. He wrote it after he awoke from a coma eleven years ago. According to him, his girlfriend—she was a professional race car driver—tried to kill him because he didn't want to marry her. She took him on a fast ride, and because she was a professional, she managed to get him hurt when they crashed but she was unscathed.

"The reason I didn't want to marry her was because I got to know her and found out she wasn't a nice person," he tells us. "And of course, that feeling was confirmed when she tried to kill me."

Together with Coma Guy's camp, the four other camps bordering our campsite form a circumference about one yard away from us on all sides. Counterclockwise next to Coma Guy is Naked Man, who hangs out on his Pathfinder in the buff, but when it comes time to take a shower he goes behind a bamboo curtain.

Next to him and closest to my camp are three nineteen-year-old women from Oregon. They spend most of their time under a tentlike structure they've created by sewing together six tapestries and placing them over oval wires that look like gigantic croquet hoops. Under their tarp they literally navel gaze: They scrutinize their belly buttons, all of which are pierced. "I used to have a really pretty belly button," one of them says staring into her now-infected navel; for a moment she looks as though she might cry.

Next over are the musicians in the RV who have spent all their money to come to Burning Man. One is a vocalist who lives in Tucson and the other is a drummer from D.C. The guy from Tucson took on an extra job at an adult video store to pay for this year's event (the $800 RV rental, the $75 tickets, etc.). "There's a company in Sedona that I came into contact with through my job at the video store that would have paid me a thousand to come here this year and just shoot videos of all the naked women walking around here, but I couldn't do that because that would violate the anticonsumer environment of Burning Man," he tells me in complete earnestness. Upon spotting Vanessa's Freud he says, "Wow, doesn't that dude write about sex and stuff?"

My quietest neighbor is a plump, bespectacled computer programmer from Oregon. He drove twenty-four hours by himself to get here, he tells me with the *Wired* magazine article tucked under his arm, and he's looking forward to meeting people. I recommend he check out the Sunscreen Camp the next day.

An unspoken schedule exists at Burning Man. At about dusk people go to their campsites to make dinner, change outfits, and put on makeup (here in Black Rock the men wear more than the women). As Vanessa and I sit outside our tent in our sun chairs and start off on the first two of our four total beers for the weekend, a twenty-year-old-looking boy with bright blue eyes and sun-kissed hair comes by and says, "How are you girls doing tonight?"

"Fine," Vanessa says.

"Do you need some Ecstasy?"

Although Burning Man is a consumer-free environment—nobody, including the organizers, is supposed to make a profit, and camps can't sell products, only "accept donations"—there's a tacit exception as far as drug sales are concerned.

We decline Blue-eyed Boy's offer and he stumbles off through the high grass to the next outside dining table. (He doesn't do RVs.) Coma Guy comes over and asks if we're doing any drugs.

"No," I tell him.

"Wow," he says. "Trippy."

The second it becomes dark, the parties begin. With them, the music starts getting louder and tiki torches suddenly abound as though it's the opening ceremony of the Olympics. We make our way to several parties—mostly raves, and to a party at a place called the Country Club, where everyone's dressed like white trash, drinking Schiltz beer and gorging themselves on family-size bags of potato chips. People at the parties do the same thing most people do at parties in Society—drink, smoke, dance—except that at Burning Man they're wearing less clothing. Walking around, I get the sense that a lot of people at Burning Man don't go to parties at home, and so lot of them act the way they think people do at parties. People who don't go to a lot of parties must think that an orgy is a requirement of any crazy party because many participants use Burning Man as an excuse to have one. These are not the choreographed orgies of X-rated movies, but rather, awkward pile-ups of people who thrash around like nonswimmers dropped into the middle of a lake. The most common sites for the so-called orgies to take place are trampolines.

Some of the things we see as we walk around the streets and into camps: a man who lights himself on fire, and a woman with a fire extinguisher who puts him out; a man with a bag of Cheetos who walks around tossing his Cheetos at people saying, "Cheeto Man blesses you"; a woman whose entire body is painted green who serves Absinthe to whoever wants to pretend they're in a Hemingway story (or whoever just wants some); and a teenage girl who climbs up onto a gigantic rocking horse that must be about twenty feet high, looks out at the metropolis of Black Rock—at the lights and the dancing and the camps crowded all together, and the thousands of people—and yells, "Oh my God, it's a mad, mad world out there."

SATURDAY

On Saturday Vanessa and I go to check out the Man, close up. Although the effigy is ostensibly the raison d'être of the Burning Man community (not to mention its namesake) no one really pays it much attention. The Man's primary function is as a navigational tool; when people give directions they say "Our camp is to the Man's right," or "The concert will be at the Main Stage, which is directly behind the Man."

When we arrive there are only three other people visiting the Man, two women who are standing on the platform between his legs having their picture taken by a third. The pilgrimage to the Man is obviously not as mandatory as one would think. The Man is merely the outline of a man, a Calderesque figure you might draw when playing hangman. His head is like a Chinese lantern, he has no feet or hands, and the only modern aspect to his otherwise archaic construction is neon tubing: blue neon outlines his body; green emphasizes his bones, including his twelve ribs. During the day the neon is turned off, and I find something sad about this, like an unplugged Christmas tree.

As Vanessa and I stand on the platform underneath the Man I see that on the inside of his right leg, where his calf would be if he had one, is an iridescent 2-by-4 inch sticker depicting Jesus on the cross. This seemingly irreverent sticker doesn't surprise me; no one at Burning Man seems to be religious—if anything, they believe in the religion of New Ageness. The Burning Man festival is like a reverse Easter weekend—it's on Sunday that the protagonist of the Burning Man religion is destroyed rather than resurrected.

More than anyone else, Larry Harvey is the preacher to this community. Although two men were responsible for the original Burning Man in 1986, the other initiator, Jerry James, decided not to be a part of Burning Man this year after the disasters that occurred at Burning Man 1996. (Among the more tragic incidents, a car ran over a tent full of people.) So Harvey is now the sole leader of the event and its spokesperson. Harvey always sports his trademark Stetson hat, and people often say he looks as though he's the sheriff of a small town, which isn't fully accurate—he looks the way a sheriff of a small town would look in a Western movie. When he talks, he keeps the back of his jaw locked, as though he's chewing on a toothpick.

On Saturday afternoon Harvey gives a speech near the cafe. His "scheduled" topic is the history of Burning Man, and I attend hoping to have my questions about the significance of the Man answered. I want to ask Harvey about similarities between Burning Man and a description of the burning of a wicker man I'd come across in Caesar's *The Conquest of Gaul*:

> As a nation the Gauls are extremely superstitious; and so persons suffering from serious diseases, as well as those who are exposed to the perils of battle, offer, or vow to offer, human sacrifices, for the performance of which they employ Druids. They believe that the only way of saving a man's life is to propitiate the gods' wrath by rendering another life in its place, and they have regular state sacrifices of the same kind. Some tribes have colossal images made of wickerwork, the limbs of which they fill with living men; they are then set on fire, and the victims burnt to death. They think that the gods prefer

the executions of men taken in the act of theft or brigandage, or guilty of some offence; but when they run short of criminals, they do not hesitate to make up with innocent men. (VI, 16)

But, I discover, everyone has their own interpretations of where Harvey must have gotten his idea from—everything from a movie called *The Wickerman* to Celtic harvest rituals are suggested as possible sources. Burning Man-ners even try to interpret Harvey's story—about how his girlfriend and he had split and he was at San Francisco's Baker Beach with some friends on the summer solstice and they decided to set fire to a man they had built out of lumber—to mean that the figure was a representation of the man his girlfriend left him for. But, Harvey maintains, there was no man she left him for; the figure represented his own human angst and it had nothing to do with her or the man. He was thirty-seven, going through a midlife crisis, and wanted something that would answer his questions about identity.

Wearing black jeans, a blue button-up shirt, and, of course, his hat, Harvey stands in front of a banner that says "Save Burning Man." He smokes a cigarette, which he ashes into a half-crushed aluminum can and tells the story of the first time he set the man on fire. "The crowd instantly doubled as the figure ignited," Harvey says, pausing dramatically. "What we had created was a community. We did it again because it had created that community, and we never stopped to give it meaning. We never said, 'This is what it represents,' we never assigned a meaning to Burning Man because we were so invested in it that it didn't need to mean anything. Burning Man has always been about immediacy. From the start people organized around it in an informal but potent way."

The authorities got involved in 1989 when over three hundred people gathered to watch the man burn at Baker Beach, and the 1990 Burning Man was moved to Black Rock, in Washoe County, Nevada. This move to the desert is what led to what Harvey calls the "Modern Burning Man," to "an experiment in community." "It was a vast desert space, a great piece of nature. It was like water, but you could walk on it," Harvey says. "You had to make a commitment to getting here and to surviving in nature. In Society you work and get your pay and buy crap so you can work. Our culture here is based on communion, not consumption. We have re-created a culture."

People at Burning Man, Harvey says, "are rootless and looking for a community, and the only way we're going to get it is if we organize a community. Like a petri dish, a culture will grow in it," he says, in all seriousness, and then immediately follows this obviously rehearsed proverb with another: "We make the hive, you make the honey."

"Like a flower," he continues, evidently on a roll, "we spread contiguously. Not like franchises, but like dandelion seeds in the wind. We plan so that this spontaneous thing that you do will just happen."

In his book *The American Religion*, Harold Bloom writes about New Age religions: "You can sometimes construe a New Age passage and hazard some guess as to more or less what some California sage hoped she or he might mean. Otherwise, the student of the New Age must be resigned to that proverbial picnic, to which the authors bring the words (or some of them, anyway) and the readers bring the meanings."

Larry Harvey certainly provides the proverbs, and is smart enough to let everyone else bring their meanings to Burning Man. He knows how desperate everyone is for it to mean *something*, but that no established meaning will suffice, especially for this crowd, who define themselves as being antirules, antisociety, and are therefore probably antirituals that have any specific significance. Harvey capitalizes on the crowd's antigovernment sentiments in his plea for money. Although the entrance fee to Burning Man more than doubled this year to $75, the operating deficit of Burning Man is $200,000 and the 1997 event costs $800,000. According to Marian Goodell, the Communications Mistress of Burning Man, the money goes to everything from Porta Potties, which cost $40,000, to the Man himself—the supplies for the Man cost $2,000; the neon, $3,000; the staff of twenty who work for two weekends before the event building the Man, almost $3,000. To satisfy safety concerns of Washoe County, Nevada commissioners, forty firefighters are on the scene at a cost of $258,000 to organizers, and it is Washoe County that Harvey rallies Burning Man-ners' antigovernment sentiments against. "We have been called locusts by the authorities of Washoe County," Harvey shouts. "We are not locusts but human beings. We need to work together."

Harvey is, of course, preaching to the converted. The crowd cheers; bike bells clink; a shirtless man wearing a straw hat and a shell necklace behind me yells out, "You can work with me, Larry."

Harvey asks everyone for a donation and says that if people give $500, they can come to Burning Man forever.

"Oh my God," the obviously stoned-out-of-his-mind guy with the shell necklace exclaims. The thought of coming to Burning Man forever is, at least at this moment, the most amazing thought to him, a dream come true.

Harvey concludes his incendiary sermon by saying, "Save Burning Man if you want to continue to see it live."

I leave without having had any of my questions about the significance of the ritual answered, but realizing that to hope for as much was to miss the point.

When I later pin down Harvey one on one, we have a long, circuitous conversation in which Harvey seems more human, less on his soap box, and more than a little overwhelmed by the cult status he has attained—people come to him for answers the way people once traveled to Lourdes for healing. I am no different. I ask him how he accounts for the fact that the figure of a man being burned shows up in so many different myths and cultures, why he thinks it touches something in our popular consciousness.

"There's a period in children's lives when they're in a state of identity formation, when they're trying to locate themselves and their place in the world and they begin drawing stick figures," Harvey says. "When you think about it, the man at Burning Man, in scale, is about how big we remember our parents when we were young. One of the ways we first realized we were ourselves was in relating to them. People relate to the figure of the Man because it is close to what they think they are. The figure of the man is our sense of individual identity made large."

If this is true, I ask Harvey, if he really believes the Man helps Burning Man-ners go through their own identity formation, how does he account for the fact that at the end of the weekend the Man is then set on fire. Again, Harvey turns to an analogy that involves a child's behavior. "The man is only useful as he enables us to go through a process. Once that process is over, we discard it as a child who, having gotten the experience he or she wanted, flings away a toy."

SUNDAY
On Sunday, I decide to get body-painted by Twinkle Fingers to show that I am, in fact, a participant. Twinkle Fingers is a masseur and body painter who is parked at an intersection by my tent. I've passed by him many times over the weekend and if I go elsewhere to get painted I'll feel like a traitor to my neighborhood. I've seen him at work with his fingers or else sleeping on his massage table, right there in the open, with one of those blindfolds they sometimes give you on airplanes over his eyes and nothing covering anything else.

"Twinkle Fingers, I presume," I say as I approach him. Hearing myself say those words I feel that maybe I have fallen through the looking glass.

"Yes?" he says.

I ask if he can do a little design on my shoulder and he sighs. "Okay," he says, less than enthusiastically, not the way you would think someone who calls himself Twinkle Fingers should say it.

Almost reluctantly, he takes out his aqua colors. Aqua colors come in little flat cylinders, like eye shadow, and Twinkle Fingers places them in a semicircle on the massage table next to where I'm sitting. Next, he backs away and stares at me as though I'm a blank canvas and he's waiting for his vision. Apparently, one comes to him because he says, "Okay, I'm ready," and he returns to the massage table. He sprays my skin with a water spritzer and then uses his fingers to spread the purple, turquoise, black, and silver paint on my skin. I can't see what he's doing but it feels like he's making a mess.

Twinkle Fingers is a little disappointed in Burning Man, he tells me, because he thought there would be more sharing. "I'm a masseur all year long—I travel around and work out of my van—and from what I read about this community everyone's supposed to bring something to share. So I brought my massage table and my paints, thinking that there would be a lot of free stuff going on. But no one else seems to be sharing."

I notice that he's using quite an excessive amount of the black paint and I wonder if this is an expression of his anger. "Don't get me wrong," he continues, "I didn't come to Burning Man expecting anything in return, I'm just a little surprised is all."

Twinkle Fingers obviously feels guilty about his lack of altruism, but I now understand his initial hesitation to paint me. He feels he's being exploited, taken advantage of, and so in return I let him paint more of my body than I had originally planned—essentially my entire upper torso save the area covered by my bikini top. When he's done, he's concerned he may have relied a little too heavily on the black and to "brighten" me up he has me stand up and take a deep breath and close my eyes and then he sprays my entire torso with silver body glitter. For days after I return from Burning Man I continue to find flecks of the silver glitter on my clothes, in my sleeping bag, in between my toes, and in my ears.

It turns out that Twinkle Fingers isn't the only one who's becoming disillusioned with Burning Man. As the day wears on, it becomes increasingly evident that the center is not holding.

I overhear a couple of fights about music among neighbors along the lines of "Would you please fucking stop afflicting us with your lack of taste in music," and I witness several altercations between bikers who, experiencing the Burning Man version of road rage, shout out, "Watch where you're going, asshole!" Near my camp, a guy's mountain bike is stolen. "That's *so* non–Burning Man," people around me say. "That's *so* not anticonsumerism."

"I think Freud was right," Vanessa says after we've been informed of the local bike theft. We're sitting outside our tent at our table and I'm using a wet rag to rub off some of what feels and looks like black lava on my skin. All I'm succeeding in doing is creating mud.

Vanessa continues, "Freud called into question the contention that civilization is largely responsible for our misery and that we would be much happier if we gave it up and returned to primitive conditions," she tells me, and pauses to hold up a gallon jug of water to her SPF 15 Chap Sticked lips and guzzle for a full minute.

"In fact, he found this contention 'astonishing,' because [she reads to me from a highlighted passage in the books], 'In whatever way we may define the concept of civilization, it is a certain fact that all the things with which we seek to protect ourselves against the threats that emanate from the sources of suffering are part of that very civilization'."

Our rocker neighbors come over ostensibly to admire my body art, but really only because there are no barriers telling them they can't just come over and interrupt us whenever they want.

Despite the increasing disgruntlement, or maybe because of it, Sunday is the most participatory day of all. Too participatory it turns out: When Vanessa goes to the Sunscreen Camp to get lotioned up, she's told that one of the volunteers was asked to leave because more than a few women complained that he was too liberal with his sunscreen application and "put sunscreen where the sun doesn't go."

One of the main attractions on Sunday is a new camp opening at 2:00 P.M. called the Grrrlie Grrrl Room. At first I think the "grrr"

spelling is derived from Riot Grrrls, punk rock girls who felt they
were being ignored by the music scene in the eighties and to show
their anger—their grrr—started writing 'zines. But the "grrr" of the
Grrrlie Grrrl Room, I discover, seems far removed from anger, and
if anything is evocative of the sounds of the camp's ample supply of
sex devices, or else the sounds that are emitted upon use of the
aforementioned supplies. The Grrrlie Grrrl Room is a group mas-
turbation room for women in honor of this year's Burning Man
theme—fertility—as though any camp at Burning Man needs an
excuse, like a theme, to revolve around sex. The entrance is a red
fur-lined, female genital-shaped opening with a white sheet hanging
down behind it for privacy. Inside the room leopard skin fabrics are
draped over beds, wicker chairs, and on the ground. There's porn-
ography to read and appliances to use. Safe sex is even a consideration: Condoms are supplied, as are plastic Ziploc baggies for the
"larger-than-life" dildos. Soft Enya-esque background music floats
through the room. It's an all-women crowd for the hour between
two and three, and when a woman is about to achieve her goal, she
is cheered on by the others. "You go, girl," a chorus chants, and
after, applauds.

At 3:00 P.M. males are allowed in the Grrrlie Grrrl room, but only
with a female hostess, and I suddenly have many male friends—
people I've met over the past few days who want to see what the
Grrrlie Grrrl Room is about and view me as their ticket in. A reporter I've met at Burning Man tries to convince me to escort him
in, but fails. Instead, I head toward Crazy Dante's Used Soul Emporium.

The way the Soul Emporium works is that you fill out a questionnaire designed to appraise your soul and then a sales representative evaluates how many points your soul is worth, and depending
on how many points you have, you can exchange your soul for
Arsenio Hall's or Hugh Grant's or whoever else at Burning Man has
already traded theirs in. (On the bulletin board where the "used
souls" are pinned I see that the reporter who was trying to coerce

me into the Grrrlie Grrrl Camp has already relinquished his.) Often, you have to barter your way for a soul and try to argue why you deserve someone else's soul, even if you don't have enough points

I sit down to answer the questionnaire, which ends up taking me a while because the questions are tough so I start with the easiest first. Question #2: *Describe the last request you absolutely refused to fulfill*. I respond: "Taking a man into the Grrrlie Grrrl Camp." The other questions force me to write down things I've done that I regret, how many people I've slept with (and if I wish the number were higher or lower), and to list any lies I've ever told. I've never before had to evaluate my life with such honesty and I can't believe it takes a Burning Man theme camp to make me do so.

When I'm finally ready to have my Soul Appraisal Questionnaire evaluated by a Personal Sales Representative, I'm told that the Used Soul Emporium is closing down for a couple of hours (even the Emporium is slacking in the participation department). So I put my questionnaire in my shorts pocket and plan on coming back. Shortly after I leave the Emporium I take the questionnaire out and unfold it to make sure my name's not on it, just in case it should fall out and into the wrong hands. It's not, so I fold it back up and restuff it in my pocket.

There's a general feeling of anticipation for the remainder of the afternoon. People are anxious for nine o'clock, when the Man is going to be set on fire. In the meantime the thought of fifteen thousand people making a grand exodus the following morning is enough to send more than a few campers packing their cars and RVs so they can make a quick getaway as soon as the Man burns.

It's the last day of Burning Man, and I'm still not sure What It All Means. Still feeling slightly cheated by the Soul Emporium, I compose my own mental questionnaire and I pass the afternoon talking to my neighbors about what the burning of the man means to them.

Sprawled on the ground near my tent talking to Coma Guy is Shawn. Stout and pallid, Shawn is wearing camouflage pants and a plaid shirt. He's focused on spinning one of the foot pedals of his Mongoose mountain bike, which is resting beside him. It turns out he knows Coma Guy from Burning Man last year. They kept up their friendship because after Burning Man each year there are Burning Man parties in warehouses in San Francisco. It's not uncommon for five hundred people to show up at these parties (they find out about it through the Internet, of course) and show their Burning Man slides (while drinking, drugging, and dancing) and talk about how great last year's Burning Man was, and how great next year's will be.

Shawn has a definite idea of what the burning of the man means: "Mankind fucks everything up, so by burning the man you're saying fuck you to society and saving the Earth." He gives the pedal of his bicycle a whirl, looks up at me and adds, "But I guess that's a pretty cliché view of it."

Another man I talk to who is in his fifties and on a bike tells me that he saves up all his anger every year and when the Man burns, his inflammatory rage turns to ashes. He's smiling while he's telling me this, and I can't help thinking that he looks like the most peaceful person at Burning Man. I tell him this, and he smiles even wider and says, "Well, it's my fifth year coming here," as though that explains everything.

The nineteen-year-old neighbor women are under their homemade tent once again. Two apply sunscreen to each other's skin—something they've been doing all weekend although they rarely emerge from the tent except at night. The third goes through an entire box of baby wipes while removing the blue body paint she was covered head to toe in the night before at a rave.

The blue girl has dyed blond hair and tells me that she came the year before hoping that she would figure out what the hell the Burning Man meant. "But I realize that the reason it works as a symbol is the same reason a poem or a book or a piece of art can be so stimulating. Everyone can interpret it how they want."

The girl who once upon a time had a pretty navel joins in. "Yeah,

I think the older something is, the more people feel that they have to give a meaning to it. It could have been totally random?"

My vocalist neighbor, who has now painted his face like some hard core Norwegian band he idolizes, shows me a video of the Daughters of Ishatar opera that took place the night before on the *playa* (the vast area beyond the campsites—the "wilderness" beyond Black Rock City). The opera ended, of course, with a big fire, which he has on tape, too. He's going to make a documentary out of the opera footage and send it to all his neighbors at Burning Man, he tells me. He's glad he taped it because he won't be able to tape it next year.

"Why not?" I ask.

"I'm going to have to sell the camera to pay for next year's trip to Burning Man."

His friend, the drummer, comes over and gives me one of his CDs. I ask him what the burning of the man will mean to him.

"It will mean it's time to go home," he says.

At seven o'clock the Society Cocktail Party begins in the center of camp. The outfits are more outrageous than usual, the stilts taller, and the drinks stronger. Even my sister seems to have undergone a conversion; in lieu of her Banana Republic halter top, she's sporting a green lei, and in her right hand is a gin and tonic. Fifteen thousand people is a lot—you see this when you look at Burning Man from the outside and mistake it for a budding metropolis—but by Sunday night's cocktail party I realize I either know or recognize a fair number of the attendees. I even run into some guys I went to high school with who are dressed as bunnies. Pink bunny suits—complete with painted-on whiskers and cottonball tails—have been their standard outfit every year they've come to Burning Man, but they wear them only on the final night, tonight, the night of the Burn. Upon spotting them, friends they've made from Burns past shout out, "Hey, it's the bunnies!" It almost feels like . . . a community.

At eight o'clock drums begin to drown out the rest of the music that's being played—even the techno music is at last defeated—and tiki torches are lit. A crowd stands around the fire pit where, for the first time this year, a solar-induced fire was started. One of the rangers explains to me that this fire is like "the eternal flame at the Olympics."

"Oh really?" I say. "How long has it been going for?"

"Since Wednesday."

"Oh."

"It's a new ritual this year," he tells me. "That's the great thing about Burning Man. I mean, look around, new rituals are being made up all the time."

Torches are lit by the fire of the fire pit, and soon I find myself in a procession of fifteen thousand people walking and dancing and chanting and drumming down the long street that leads to the figure of the Man. The Man alternates between flashing just his twelve green ribs and then his full blue and green colors.

Something amazing happens as fifteen thousand people make their way toward the Man. Both his arms, which have been by his side all weekend long, rise up at the same time. They keep rising up until they are above his lantern head. The crowd goes even crazier if this is possible, the drums get even louder, and the chanting becomes contagious, like a song you can't get out of your head, and suddenly I find myself singing, too.

Above the din of fifteen thousand people, I hear the man next to me say to his female companion, "You have two minutes to decide what this ritual means to you."

"Oh God," she says, panicking under the pressure.

In my dash to the front of the crowd, I've become separated from my sister and my bunny friends. I look around for them and instead see waving rubber chickens and cows and swans, Burning Man versions of animals to be sacrificed.

People start yelling, "Burn the Man!" and one guy walks around with an electronic display that flashes red letters that say "Burn!"

The fire marshals and the Burning Man Project volunteers miraculously stop the crowd from getting too close and manage to make everyone form a gigantic semicircle around the Man, at a distance of about thirty feet back from him. I know this because I'm up front.

Suddenly, a guy in shorts and dyed blond hair runs from the base of the man, ducking fire patrollers and slides in next to me like a baseball player sliding into home. His name is Secret, he tells me, when he catches his breath.

"Why are you called Secret?" I ask.

"I can't tell you," he says.

Secret is good-looking in a *Dawson's Creek* kind of way. In a non–*Dawson's Creek* way, he's wearing black eyeliner beneath his wide eyes and an attached set of five eight-inch-long nails on his right hand. The claw has batteries and is lit up a glow-in-the-dark red. I tap one of the red fingers the way you tap an iron, expecting it to be hot, but it's not.

"Cool," I say.

"I hate that man," he tells me.

For a moment, I think he's talking about someone sitting near us, but then I see that he's staring at the forty-foot Man. The neon from the effigy lights up Secret's eyes and they do, in fact, look like angry eyes.

"Why do you hate him?"

"Why? Because he represents everything I'm angry about."

"What are you angry about?"

"Society. Corporate America. The media." He turns his angelic face to me and says, "What are you angry about?"

"Me? Nothing." I feel like a Spectator.

We talk a little more and Secret tells me he is twenty-one and from a small town outside of Sacramento. He heard about Burning Man from all the raves he goes to in San Francisco, and this is his third year coming back. He thinks they should have Burning Man twice a year because once a year isn't enough.

"Are you sacrificing anything to the Man?" he says.

"What?"

"Did you put anything underneath the man?" he says.

It occurs to me that this is what he was doing before he sprinted past the fire marshals and dove in beside me.

"No," I say. "What are you sacrificing?"

"Pizza."

"Large or small or a slice?" I ask.

"A large box."

"Pepperoni?"

"No," Secret tells me. "It was just the box."

"Just the box?" I say.

"Yeah."

"Why?"

"Because I work for Godfather's Pizza and I hate my job. I'm sacrificing that box so that with it I can burn all my anger."

"Corporate America," I say.

"Yeah," he says. "You understand." He looks at me lovingly, this angry boy, and then he takes his red claw and massages my now dirt-and-dry-heat dread-locked hair with them. It feels good and I'm enjoying this weird Freddy Kruger version of a head massage and I'm feeling very relaxed until someone behind us yells, "Burn him."

And then it happens.

A man is set on fire. Not the man you're thinking of, but a real man is set on fire in between the Burning Man's legs. Eventually he is extinguished, and the Burning Man himself is ignited with the help of diesel (past years have proven gasoline to be too volatile). He starts to burn simultaneously at the end of each limb.

Everyone is cheering or drumming and going wild. The fire races up the Man's legs, more quickly up his left; and down his arms, more quickly down his right. Catching fire, the neon tubes start emitting a sizzling sound, not unlike the sound of three million mosquitoes being simultaneously zapped.

The burning goes on for forty-five minutes; I'm so mesmerized it seems like only two. The sky is lit orange from the glow, and so are everyone's faces around me. When the entire frame of the Man has finally been weakened, he falls forward a little, as though he's received a hard punch in the stomach, and then he starts to fall back. It is the most alive the Man has seemed, his body moving as though his joints can rotate. He finally falls to his left, and then to the ground with a crash and sparks.

Fifteen thousand people scream. Everyone around me jumps up, as though to assert their triumph: The man has fallen and they are standing. The entire night sky looks like it's been eclipsed by the sun, and there is a flame where there once was a man, and orange sparks shoot up into the sky and out like fireworks. Some spiraling-downward sizzling sparks land on my arm and burn, proof that I am really here.

I find myself jumping up and down with adrenaline and the beauty of a lit sky in a wide desert. For the first time, I truly feel a part of this community and suddenly I understand the strange beauty of this even stranger ritual. On the verge of being knocked over by the chaos and excitement of it all, I grab onto something to steady me. I'm holding on for I don't know how long when I realize that I've locked fingers with Secret's glowing claw.

"Let's dance around it," Secret says, and pulls my hand with his claws. Secret is a veteran Burning Man-ner and my Virgil to the Inferno-esque ritual. He knows that once the man falls, everyone dances around him, one time, two times, all night.

I'm still (and even more inexplicably since I'm now conscious of it) holding tight onto his red claw when he asks me if I've heard of Herakleitos. At first I think he must be talking about a rave in San Francisco (he's already told me that he's heard the rave scene in New York is beat and feels bad for me that I don't live near the good raves, i.e., the ones in San Francisco). But it turns out he is, in fact, taking about the Greek philosopher.

"Herakleitos is the man!" Secret says. "Have you read what he's said about fire? He says it's passion and everything around us. That's what Burning Man is all about, that's what this fire is all about. It's all about passion."

Having incited passion, Secret leans over, and holding the small of my back with his claw, he kisses me. I feel myself pulling away, I hear myself telling him I have a boyfriend.

"Did you know that Larry Harvey first burned the Man to represent the guy his girlfriend left him for?" Secret says.

I want to explain to Secret that this isn't quite the case, but it's what Secret chooses to believe (along with the idea that the Man represents society, corporate America, the media, et al.) so I nod. He lets me go and holds up his red claw as though to assure me, Okay, claw off. It's awkward between us—isn't separation always that way?—and I look around for an exit from the situation. What's transpired is the opposite of what's supposed to happen when a couple kisses in movies—the Kiss after which the music swells, the colors brighten, and everything in the world is right because Love has been found.

Instead, I feel ill.

I feel alone, so *not* a part of any community that there must be a word for it—*de*communitized—and something else. The sense that rather than having had an epiphany about Burning Man, what I was really experiencing was a moment of temporary insanity. I was caught up in the moment, the fifteen thousand people, the fire. I was caught up, so desperately, in the desire for it to mean something, for it all to mean something.

I think back on what Larry Harvey said to me, that the man is only useful as he enables us to go through a process of identity formation and that once that process is over, we discard it as a child who, having gotten the experience he or she wanted, flings away a toy. Is this the case with all rituals, I wonder?

Of course, Burning Man is different from other rituals I've focused on because it's not exclusive to young women. But, like many of the initiations young women go through today, Burning Man is about having an identity within a community, about having a place in the world. After spending the long weekend trying to make the metamorphosis from spectator to participant, and observing others do the same, and then watching the Man, the figure people have travelled from around the world to be united by, burn to ashes, I can't help thinking, What happens after young women go through the ritual that they think will make them belong? What next?

In the distance I spot my sister and our bunny friends and when I catch up to them, we take a walk on the *playa*. The night is warm and the sky is the color of autumnal leaves. We go to glow-in-the-dark discos, and to parties, and to concerts, and watch women spinning tiki torches around with the same hand motions they'd use to jump rope.

We go to a camp called Circus X and watch topless women twirling batons. Topless women have been twirling batons all weekend long whether at the circus or not and the crowd becomes restless. "Burn it!" someone yells, and other incendiaries join in to form a chorus. It's not clear what they want to have burned. Just something. *Anything.* It's gotten to the point where fire is the only show people want to watch. Nearby, an objet d'art is torched and everyone abandons the circus for the flames.

In the dark and because it is on fire, it's difficult to make out exactly what is being burned, but I'm fairly certain it's the wooden Trojan Horse sculpture I've passed by several times. The fire is as big as a tall, fat tree, and suddenly there are a hundred naked and clothed people crowded around it.

We roam like nomads from one fire to another, and soon find ourselves lost. With no Burning Man at the center of the city, it's difficult to determine one's position in the camp. To further complicate matters, cars and vans have already started leaving, so landmarks like buses and U-Hauls—once our signposts in this makeshift community—have left only dirt where once there was direction.

Others, it seems, are not as lost, for when Vanessa and I say goodbye to the bunnies and travel toward where we think we'll find our car, we see approximately fifty people gathered around a bright white light. The image reminds me of a photograph I once saw of winter-parka-bundled people huddled around a light at the North Pole, trying to catch a bit of artificial sunlight in the dark days of winter.

But this light is different. It's just a white light in the middle of the desert that slowly spins like a barber's pole. Amazed, Vanessa and I continue to watch as it becomes later and later, and not one of the fifty observers moves: they all lay on their stomachs, some staring straight at the light, others observing it through the lens of their videocameras. At first we find this amusing, even laughable—all these video cameras will come back from Burning Man with hours of footage of a white light going around and around in circles.

But later, once we have found our car and miraculously made our way out of the ghost town that Black Rock City has become and onto the highway, I'm driving on into the dark, into nowhere, in silence because Vanessa's sleeping in the passenger seat, and I find myself surprisingly saddened by the image. All these people who want so desperately to be a part of a community, to have their identity defined by that community, that even when the ritual that has brought them together is over, when its central signifier has literally been burned to the ground, they search for something else, for anything—even if it's merely a white light—around which they can gather together again.

ACKNOWLEDGMENTS

This book would not have been possible without the support and talents of so many people. In particular, I wish to thank:

My agent, Mary Evans, for giving these words paper and my editor, Reagan Arthur, for her skills at rearranging them. Also, Tanya McKinnon at Mary Evans Inc. for all her hard work.

My teachers, for their encouragement and knowledge, especially Julia Alvarez, David Bain, Robert Pack, and Richard Locke.

Sarah Stewart Taylor for her suggestions and criticisms. To have such a talented writer and editor as such a good friend makes me feel truly fortunate. Joshua Pashman for years of exchanging words—both verbal and written; Alexandra Flynn for her enthusiasm; Ninive Clements for her ideas; Robert Kessel because I promised; Shannon Herbert for her research assistance; Jack Martinez, Michael Beckwith, and Matthew Yeoman for their help setting up interviews in their respective cities, and both the Beckwith and Yeoman families for not just giving me places to stay, but making me feel at home during my travels for this book.

And more than I can express, Jacob Waletzky.